MUHAMMAD ALI

MUHAMMAD ALI

Jack Rummel

Senior Consulting Editor
Nathan Irvin Huggins
Director
W.E.B. Du Bois Institute for Afro-American Research
Harvard University

CHELSEA HOUSE PUBLISHERS
New York   Philadelphia

Editor-in-Chief   Nancy Toff

Executive Editor   Remmel T. Nunn

Managing Editor   Karyn Gullen Browne

Copy Chief   Juliann Barbato

Picture Editor   Adrian G. Allen

Art Director   Giannella Garrett

Manufacturing Manager   Gerald Levine

Staff for MUHAMMAD ALI

Senior Editor   Richard Rennert

Associate Editor   Perry King

Assistant Editor   Gillian Bucky

Copy Editor   Karen Hammonds

Editorial Assistant   Susan DeRosa

Associate Picture Editor   Juliette Dickstein

Picture Researcher   Emily Miller

Senior Designer   Laurie Jewell

Design Assistant   Laura Lang

Production Coordinator   Joseph Romano

Cover Illustration   Alan J. Nahigian

Creative Director   Harold Steinberg

15 14 13 12 11

Library of Congress Cataloging in Publication Data

Rummel, Jack.
   Muhammad Ali.

   (Black Americans of achievement)
   Bibliography: p.
   Summary: Chronicles the life of the heavyweight boxing
champion, from his early years to his draft resistance through
his astounding boxing career, which established him as one
of the greatest fighters of all time.
   1. Ali, Muhammad, 1942–   —Juvenile literature.
2. Boxers (Sports)—United States—Biography—Juvenile
literature. [1. Ali, Muhammad, 1942– . 2. Boxers
(Sports). 3. Afro-Americans—Biography] I. Title.
II. Series.
GV1132.A44R86   1988   796.8'3'0924 [B] [92]   87-29962
ISBN 1-55546-569-2
      0-7910-0210-1 (pbk.)

CONTENTS

On Achievement 7
Coretta Scott King

1
Miss Velvet Green 11

2
Cassius Clay of Louisville 15

3
Dance of the Dinosaurs 27

4
A Call from Islam 41

5
A Technical Knockout 55

6
The Exile 65

7
Resurrection of a Heavyweight 77

8
The Greatest 95

9
The Champion of Change 109

Chronology 123

Further Reading 124

Index 125

BLACK AMERICANS OF ACHIEVEMENT

RALPH ABERNATHY
civil rights leader

MUHAMMAD ALI
heavyweight champion

RICHARD ALLEN
religious leader and social activist

LOUIS ARMSTRONG
musician

ARTHUR ASHE
tennis great

JOSEPHINE BAKER
entertainer

JAMES BALDWIN
author

BENJAMIN BANNEKER
scientist and mathematician

AMIRI BARAKA
poet and playwright

COUNT BASIE
bandleader and composer

ROMARE BEARDEN
artist

JAMES BECKWOURTH
frontiersman

MARY MCLEOD BETHUNE
educator

BLANCHE BRUCE
politician

RALPH BUNCHE
diplomat

GEORGE WASHINGTON CARVER
botanist

CHARLES CHESNUTT
author

BILL COSBY
entertainer

PAUL CUFFE
merchant and abolitionist

FATHER DIVINE
religious leader

FREDERICK DOUGLASS
abolitionist editor

CHARLES DREW
physician

W.E.B. DU BOIS
scholar and activist

PAUL LAURENCE DUNBAR
poet

KATHERINE DUNHAM
dancer and choreographer

MARIAN WRIGHT EDELMAN
civil rights leader and lawyer

DUKE ELLINGTON
bandleader and composer

RALPH ELLISON
author

JULIUS ERVING
basketball great

JAMES FARMER
civil rights leader

ELLA FITZGERALD
singer

MARCUS GARVEY
black-nationalist leader

DIZZY GILLESPIE
musician

PRINCE HALL
social reformer

W. C. HANDY
father of the blues

WILLIAM HASTIE
educator and politician

MATTHEW HENSON
explorer

CHESTER HIMES
author

BILLIE HOLIDAY
singer

JOHN HOPE
educator

LENA HORNE
entertainer

LANGSTON HUGHES
poet

ZORA NEALE HURSTON
author

JESSE JACKSON
civil rights leader and politician

JACK JOHNSON
heavyweight champion

JAMES WELDON JOHNSON
author

SCOTT JOPLIN
composer

BARBARA JORDAN
politician

MARTIN LUTHER KING, JR.
civil rights leader

ALAIN LOCKE
scholar and educator

JOE LOUIS
heavyweight champion

RONALD MCNAIR
astronaut

MALCOLM X
militant black leader

THURGOOD MARSHALL
Supreme Court justice

ELIJAH MUHAMMAD
religious leader

JESSE OWENS
champion athlete

CHARLIE PARKER
musician

GORDON PARKS
photographer

SIDNEY POITIER
actor

ADAM CLAYTON POWELL, JR.
political leader

LEONTYNE PRICE
opera singer

A. PHILIP RANDOLPH
labor leader

PAUL ROBESON
singer and actor

JACKIE ROBINSON
baseball great

BILL RUSSELL
basketball great

JOHN RUSSWURM
publisher

SOJOURNER TRUTH
antislavery activist

HARRIET TUBMAN
antislavery activist

NAT TURNER
slave revolt leader

DENMARK VESEY
slave revolt leader

MADAM C. J. WALKER
entrepreneur

BOOKER T. WASHINGTON
educator

HAROLD WASHINGTON
politician

WALTER WHITE
civil rights leader and author

RICHARD WRIGHT
author

ON ACHIEVEMENT

Coretta Scott King

BEFORE YOU BEGIN this book, I hope you will ask yourself what the word excellence means to you. I think that it's a question we should all ask, and keep asking as we grow older and change. Because the truest answer to it should never change. When you think of excellence, perhaps you think of success at work; or of becoming wealthy; or meeting the right person, getting married, and having a good family life.

Those important goals are worth striving for, but there is a better way to look at excellence. As Martin Luther King, Jr., said in one of his last sermons, "I want you to be first in love. I want you to be first in moral excellence. I want you to be first in generosity. If you want to be important, wonderful. If you want to be great, wonderful. But recognize that he who is greatest among you shall be your servant."

My husband, Martin Luther King, Jr., knew that the true meaning of achievement is service. When I met him, in 1952, he was already ordained as a Baptist preacher and was working towards a doctoral degree at Boston University. I was studying at the New England Conservatory and dreamed of accomplishments in music. We married a year later, and after I graduated the following year we moved to Montgomery, Alabama. We didn't know it then, but our notions of achievement were about to undergo a dramatic change.

You may have read or heard about what happened next. What began with the boycott of a local bus line grew into a national movement, and by the time he was assassinated in 1968 my husband had fashioned a black movement powerful enough to shatter forever the practice of racial segregation. What you may not have read about is where he got his method for resisting injustice without compromising his religious beliefs.

He got the strategy of nonviolence from a man of a different race, who lived in a distant country, and even practiced a different religion. The man was Mahatma Gandhi, the great leader of India, who devoted his life to serving humanity in the spirit of love and nonviolence. It was in these principles that Martin discovered his method for social reform. More than anything else, those two principles were the key to his achievements.

This book is about black Americans who served society through the excellence of their achievements. It forms a part of the rich history of black men and women in America—a history of stunning accomplishments in every field of human endeavor, from literature and art to science, industry, education, diplomacy, athletics, jurisprudence, even polar exploration.

Not all of the people in this history had the same ideals, but I think you will find something that all of them have in common. Like Martin Luther King, Jr., they all decided to become "drum majors" and serve humanity. In that principle—whether it was expressed in books, inventions, or song—they found something outside themselves to use as a goal and a guide. Something that showed them a way to serve others, instead of living only for themselves.

Reading the stories of these courageous men and women not only helps us discover the principles that we will use to guide our own lives, but it teaches us about our black heritage and about America itself. It is crucial for us to know the heroes and heroines of our history and to realize that the price we paid in our struggle for equality in America was dear. But we must also understand that we have gotten as far as we have partly because America's democratic system and ideals made it possible.

We still are struggling with racism and prejudice. But the great men and women in this series are a tribute to the spirit of our democratic ideals and the system in which they have flourished. And that makes their stories special, and worth knowing. ✺

MUHAMMAD
ALI

1

MISS
VELVET
GREEN

❧

O N A WARM and humid day on April 28, 1967, Muhammad Ali, the heavyweight boxing champion of the world, does not go to the gym for a workout. Instead, the 25-year-old fighter makes his way to the federal courthouse in Houston, Texas. Ali, whose legal residence is the state of Kentucky rather than Texas, has nonetheless come to know Houston quite well: Only two months earlier, he fought and won a brutal 15-round match against Ernie Terrell in Houston's Astrodome; and three months before that, in November 1966, he fought Cleveland Williams in an easier match at that same venue. However, Ali is not in Houston on this spring day to fight any one man. He has been summoned to Texas to report for induction into the armed forces of the United States of America.

A large crowd of onlookers has gathered at the courthouse by the time Ali and his lawyers arrive. A mob of reporters and photographers rush him as he gets out of a taxi at the foot of the courthouse steps. These spectators have not come to wish him well at the beginning of a stint in the army. Instead, they are there either to support or vilify him as he is about to tell U.S. Selective Service Board officials that he is not destined to become just another GI. He has

Ali's brash and colorful style has made him a center of controversy as well as one of the most popular figures in the world of sports.

While weighing in for a heavy-weight championship fight on February 6, 1967, at the Astrodome in Houston, Texas, Ali stares down his opponent, Ernie Terrell (right), in an attempt to upset his concentration.

already promised in public to refuse induction into the army, thus risking for himself a long jail sentence and the possible ruin of his professional career.

Ali is bombarded with questions as he and his entourage—his bodyguards and aides—mount the courthouse steps. A group of black students from Texas Southern University march back and forth across the street. From behind police barricades, they shout their support for Ali and hold up signs that demand, "Stay Home, Muhammad Ali." A group of hippies also yell support for him. Other bystanders are not so sympathetic.

At the top of the courthouse steps, Ali is joined by one of his trainers, Drew "Bundini" Brown. While the crowd of reporters jostle around them, Brown, who is known simply as Bundini, gestures across the street. "There she is now," he says.

Ali's gaze searches the crowd until he finds her. He has seen her before; she has been haunting him on his recent trips to Houston. She is a stylish white woman, perhaps 40 years old. With her is a chauffeur and another man. As before, she is wearing a dress of green velvet.

Ali's most vivid memory of this woman is from after his tough and bloody fight with Terrell. That night, as he made his way through the crowd after the fight, she appeared before him with pen and paper and asked for his autograph. Ali clearly remembered her face from after his recent fight with Williams.

"I come to all your fights," the woman he has since named Miss Velvet Green said to him. "I will keep coming," she continued as she neatly folded the paper containing the autograph he had given her, "until I see them take you out on a stretcher. God won't always let evil win."

For Ali, this nameless woman in the green velvet dress has come to personify the hatred directed toward him because of his exuberant style, personal beliefs, and religious convictions. For every man or woman cheering for him to win in or out of the ring, there is a Miss Velvet Green hoping to see him knocked out, sent to prison, or even killed. These intense feelings have been aroused because Ali is more than just another heavyweight champion. For some, he is a symbol of black pride; for others, he is an example of the kind of courage one must have if one is to protest against an unpopular war; and for many more— including Miss Velvet Green—he is the incarnation of threatening and unwanted social change.

She stands on the other side of the street, waiting until Ali spots her. Then, assured that she has been noticed by him, she begins to leave. Her figure in green is the last thing that Ali sees before he turns around to confront the power of the U.S. government. ❧

Displaying a publication issued by fellow Black Muslims, Ali discusses the injustice of having to serve in the army when it goes against one's religious beliefs.

2
CASSIUS CLAY OF LOUISVILLE

MUHAMMAD ALI WAS born into a working-class household in Louisville, Kentucky, on January 18, 1942. He was originally named Cassius Marcellus Clay, Jr., after both his father and a prominent 19th-century abolitionist and politician. He legally changed his name to Muhammad Ali from Cassius Clay when he was 21 years old.

The eldest of two sons, Cassius was part of a closely knit and loving family. His mother, Odessa Grady Clay, was affectionately called Bird by her family. She worked as a cook and housecleaner. His father, Cassius, Sr., was known as Cash. He worked as a sign painter to support his family. He also painted murals on the walls of black churches around Louisville to earn additional money and to exercise his artistic talent.

By all accounts, Cash Clay was a warm-hearted man. He had a bit of an actor in him, and he loved to sing. In the family's home at night, he would imitate his favorite crooners: Nat "King" Cole, Bing Crosby, and Russ Colombo. His love for the entertainment world eventually prompted him to name his second son Rudolph Valentino Clay after the popular silent film star.

Watching his father at work and at play, young Cassius sensed that despite his apparent gaiety, his father felt frustrated. He was someone with the ability

While Ali was growing up in Louisville, Kentucky, his rise to the top of the boxing world was aided by his brother, Rudy (left).

15

Ali's mother, Odessa (shown here), worked hard to create a warm and loving family life that instilled a great sense of confidence and security in her prizefighting son.

to be more than just a sign painter. In another city or at another time, he might have been able to become a successful artist. However, opportunities for blacks were limited in Louisville. He was only offered the chance to paint on church walls, on the sides of buildings, and on large billboards.

The future heavyweight champion made a vow early on to leave the South. He wanted more out of life than a place such as Louisville could give him.

While black workers in Kentucky were not very well paid, the Clays were neither the poorest nor the wealthiest of black families in Louisville. They never went hungry, yet there was seldom any money left over for items that many American families took for granted. Hamburgers and hot dogs were standard fare at the dinner table; chicken and potatoes were considered extravagances. The family's clothes were always secondhand. The four-room house in which they lived was in constant need of repair. The roof leaked and the porch was in danger of falling down, but the

During Ali's childhood, his father, Cash (shown here), worked as a sign painter. Although he was a skilled artist, he was given few chances to display his artistic talents in the racially discriminatory South.

money that Cassius's parents earned went for essential items first: food, clothing, bills, a used car, and gasoline. After paying for these basic needs, they usually did not have any money left.

Cassius and his brother, Rudy, did own bicycles, but even these were necessities. Their parents did not have enough money for the two boys to take a bus to school, so they rode their bikes instead.

The Clays lived in Louisville's West End section, which was one of the city's three black ghettos. When Cassius was growing up, there were laws in many states that were aimed specifically at keeping blacks and whites separated. Known as Jim Crow laws, they forbade blacks such as Cassius from going into certain stores to buy groceries or refreshments or into certain theaters to see a movie. These laws also established many separate facilities for blacks and whites, including schools and hotels. In downtown Louisville, blacks were allowed to shop in department stores but were not allowed to eat in the store cafeterias. Nor

Fourteen-year-old Emmett Till (shown here) was lynched in 1955 by three men who probably belonged to the Ku Klux Klan, a white supremacist organization. Till's death deeply upset Ali, who was almost the same age as the murdered youth.

were they allowed to eat in many of the cafés or restaurants in the city's main commercial area. Not surprisingly, such restrictions caused feelings of resentment among many blacks.

Cassius's childhood was filled with incidents in which he was denied entrance to a place where whites were allowed to go. By the time he was a teenager attending DuValle Junior High School, he felt compelled to react against the pressure of being a black in a predominantly white society. His actions were touched off by a story that he heard in 1955 about the murder of a 14 year old from Chicago named Emmett Till.

While Till was visiting his uncle in Mississippi during a summer vacation, he was beaten, shot, and thrown into a river by three white men who may have been members of the white supremacist organization known as the Ku Klux Klan. They had abducted Till because his appearance matched the description of a young black who had "spoken to" a white woman. (The men claimed that Till had made sexual advances to the woman.) Yet they denied killing him—even though a number of witnesses offered damning evidence against them. The men were tried by an all-white jury in Mississippi and were found not guilty of Till's murder; a grand jury also refused to indict them on the charge of kidnapping.

The purpose of such lynchings was to frighten blacks throughout America into remaining in a position of economic and social subservience. However, Till's mother fought this vicious strategy. To confront the Klan as well as to provoke outrage against the kind of men who would murder an unarmed and innocent boy, she displayed her son's mutilated body as it lay at rest in an open casket. Thousands of people—many of them total strangers to the family—came to pay their respects to the young man and to show their support for his mother and the cause of

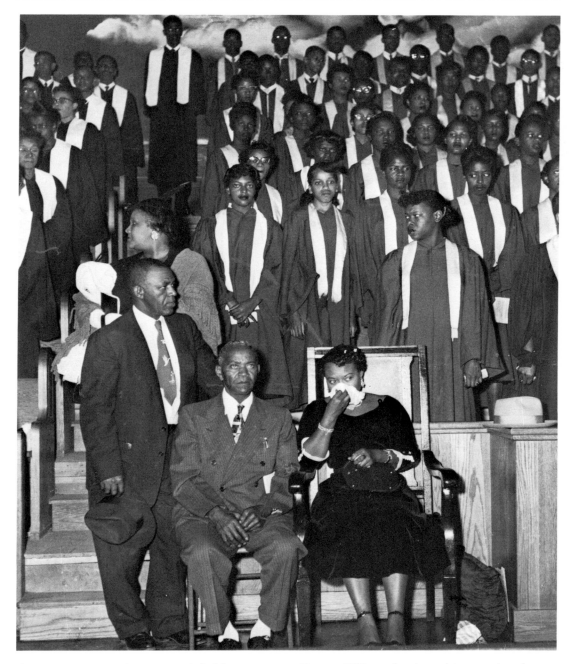

A major moment in the growing civil rights movement: Emmett Till's mother (seated in center) and members of New York City's black community protest the acquittal of Till's alleged murderers in 1955.

racial justice. Her actions were one of the first public expressions of outrage in what would become known as the civil rights movement.

The news of this horrible crime was given extensive coverage in the press, particulary in the black newspapers around the country. The story deeply affected Cassius, whose emotions ranged from shock to sadness to anger. He soon felt a need to strike back at white society, which he held responsible for Till's death. Not knowing what to do—although feeling the need to act, no matter in how futile or pointless a way—he sneaked out of his house one night and met up with a friend at the West End railroad station. The two boys placed some pieces of metal on some of the tracks in the hope of derailing a train.

After doing this, Cassius noticed a poster nailed to a lamppost. The image displayed on the poster infuriated him, and he began hurling stones at the poster until it was ripped to pieces. The poster had shown a stern, elderly white man with a long, wispy white beard: "Uncle Sam," the symbol of the U.S. government. Below his visage were the words "I Want You." The poster was a recruiting advertisement for the U.S. Army.

Cassius's actions at the train station were largely out of character; throughout his youth, he kept out of trouble and attended school regularly. Yet he and Till had been about the same age, so to Cassius there seemed no reason other than pure chance as to why Till had been killed and he had not. He was beginning to discover—as many teenagers do—that the world is a place where grave injustices can be committed.

A similar discovery took place on an afternoon in 1954, the year before Till's death. Cassius was riding on a new bicycle, accompanied by his friend Johnny Willis. His bike was a Schwinn, with red lights, chrome trim, and whitewall tires. It had been given to him for Christmas by his father.

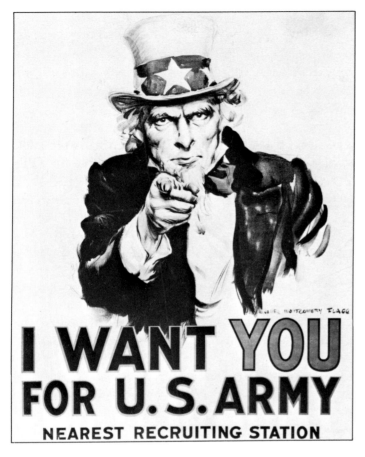

When Ali was 13 years old, he became enraged at a U.S. Army recruitment poster, which he viewed as a symbol of white-ruled America. The budding fighter would have a significant encounter with the army in the following decade.

On that day, the two boys were riding up and down the streets of Louisville with no particular purpose in mind. When it began to rain, they rode over to the Columbia Auditorium to dry off. Willis knew that a bazaar called the Louisville Home Show was being held in the auditorium and that free hot dogs, popcorn, and candy were being served there.

Cassius and his friend stayed at the auditorium for part of the afternoon. When they left the building to return home, Cassius discovered that his bicycle had been stolen. He immediately became upset; he was not looking forward to telling his father what had happened. Consequently, he rushed around the neighborhood, trying unsuccessfully to locate his bike.

Someone finally directed Cassius to a white policeman named Joe Martin, who ran a boxing program in the Columbia Auditorium gym, which was across the street from Nazareth College, where Cassius worked part-time. In the gym, Martin wrote down what the boy told him about the theft. However, by the end of their interview, Cassius had nearly forgotten his troubles. The scene inside the gym, which was filled with boxers jumping rope, shadow boxing, and popping the speed bags, mesmerized him. Martin must have noticed this, for he gave Cassius an application to join the boxing program, which ran from six to eight o'clock in the evening, Monday through Friday.

Cassius took an application form but did not make a decision about joining the program until the following Saturday. That afternoon, he happened to tune in to a local television show called "Tomorrow's Champions," which featured amateur boxing matches in Louisville. There on television, working as a manager and trainer in the corner of one of the boxers, was Joe Martin from the Columbia gym. Impressed by seeing Martin on television, Cassius pointed him out to his parents and told them that he wanted to give boxing a try. Although they were a little hesitant, they agreed to let him start training.

Not quite yet 13 years old, Cassius began his boxing career as a skinny 112-pound novice. His first sparring match was with an older and more experienced opponent who bounced enough punches off of Cassius's head to leave him dizzy, discouraged, and bleeding from the nose. After fighting for a few rounds, another young fighter came up to him and offered a few words of advice. "Don't box these older fellows first," he said. "Box the fellows who are new like you. Get someone to teach you how to do it."

Cassius started to learn what he could about boxing. Although he was a novice, his tremendous stamina helped him wear down his opponents. He was

Ali first started to take boxing lessons when he was 12 years old. He learned his lessons so well that one year later he was making appearances on a television program featuring top amateur boxers.

soon making appearances on "Tomorrow's Champions," and even though he was still an amateur fighter, he was paid four dollars for each appearance on the show. To a poor young fighter in 1955, this amount was a lot of money.

That same year, Cassius made it to the Kentucky State Golden Gloves championship tournament. In the tournament, he was beaten by a fighter from a rival gym in Louisville—the Grace Community Center gym—who was managed by Fred Stoner. Soon after Cassius was defeated in this tournament, he started to train with Stoner as well as with Martin.

Cassius quickly developed a regular daily schedule. He went to school from eight in the morning until two in the afternoon, then worked for the Catholic sisters in the library of Nazareth College until six in the evening. After grabbing a quick bite to eat, he would train at Martin's gym until eight, then he would fine-tune his boxing skills at Stoner's until midnight. It was important for Cassius to set a strict schedule for himself. In order to become a champion boxer—which is what he was aiming to become—a fighter had to have a lot of discipline.

Although Cassius trained hard with Martin, he trained even harder with Stoner, who not only emphasized the fine points of counterpunching but also demanded that his boxers work on basic conditioning. Consequently, Cassius ran many miles every day and did sit-ups until his abdominal muscles hurt so much that he could not do any more. Then, for good measure, he played catch with a medicine ball so he could strengthen his midsection even more and jumped rope until his legs became extremely tired. As a result of this training, he began to win . . . 50 fights . . . 100 fights. Before long, he had won 161 amateur fights out of 167. Of the six fights that he lost, most took place at the beginning of his amateur career.

By the time Cassius entered Central High School, he was a seasoned amateur boxer as well as a student. One day, a teacher noted his name approvingly by saying, "Cassius Marcellus Clay, if only you could just follow in the footsteps of that great friend of Abraham Lincoln, that fighting Abolitionist whose name you carry. . . ." Until then, Cassius had never given much thought to his name, which he knew was also the name of a white Kentucky-born abolitionist who had lived in the 19th century.

Spurred on by his teacher's comment, Cassius discovered that the abolitionist Clay was a member of the aristocracy and a close relative of Senator Henry Clay's. Although he had inherited slaves and large holdings of land from his father, he eventually denounced the institution of slavery. He freed his slaves shortly before the Civil War and ran for Congress as a crusader against slavery. Even though he was defeated in his bid for Congress, he continued his abolitionist efforts. He founded an abolitionist newspaper, the *True American*, and in 1854, he helped found the Republican party, which under Abraham Lincoln became the party that legally ended slavery in the United States.

However, as the future heavyweight champion dug further into the facts about Clay's life, he discovered some disquieting information. Although Clay was opposed to slavery, he did not believe that blacks were the equals of whites. In a collection of Clay's writings, Cassius found the following:

> I am of the opinion that the Caucasian or white is the superior race; they have a larger and a better formed brain; much more developed form and exquisite structure. Modern discovery proved that the builders of pyramids and Egyptian founders of signs and letters were white. . . .

Clay was a much more complicated and difficult person than the simple hero that Cassius was led to believe. Rather than being a true champion of racial equality, he was something of a racist. Although he had freed his slaves, he had not succeeded in freeing his mind from misguided yet popular opinion. The high school student Cassius Clay would remember this distinction. Although he said little about his discovery to his acquaintances, his given name would never sound so fine to him again. ❧

Although abolitionist Cassius Marcellus Clay (shown here) embarked on a crusade in the 19th century to end slavery, he did not believe in racial equality. Ali became deeply disturbed when he discovered this sad truth about the person whose name he bore.

3
DANCE
OF THE
DINOSAURS

❦

PROFESSIONAL BOXING IS divided into eight weight classes: flyweight, bantamweight, featherweight, lightweight, welterweight, middleweight, light heavyweight, and heavyweight. Fighters from the heavyweight division are the ones who have most consistently grabbed the attention of the public. Perhaps it is because they are the biggest men, the gladiators; perhaps it is because their division has produced the most colorful fighters. Whatever the reason, the heavyweight champions stand at the pinnacle of boxing, and their names have the ring of poetry to the ears of boxing fans: John L. Sullivan, "Gentleman Jim" Corbett, Jack Johnson, Gene Tunney, Jack Dempsey, Joe Louis, Rocky Marciano. . . .

Even when Cassius Clay was a 112-pound 13-year-old flyweight, he dreamed of one day becoming the heavyweight champion. As soon as he began training as a fighter, he learned that heavyweights had a mystique about them that was all their own. Boxing fans simply paid more attention to heavyweight championship bouts than to any other fights.

The electricity that surrounds a world heavyweight championship fight was first brought home to Clay when he happened to overhear a broadcast of such a match. He was all alone, walking to Stoner's gym, when he spotted a group of people clustered

John L. Sullivan battles Jack Kilrain on July 8, 1889, in the last heavyweight bout to be fought with bare knuckles.

around a parked car whose radio was broadcasting a championship fight that was in progress. Clay went over to the car and elbowed a spot for himself next to a door so he could hear more clearly. The fight was a fierce contest, and the group huddled around the car was excited by it.

Suddenly, one of the boxers scored a knockout, and the fight was over. "The winner," the ringside announcer said, "and still heavyweight champion of the world, Rocky Marciano."

"And still heavyweight champion of the world . . ." These words rang magically in Clay's ears and left him without any doubts: He wanted to be a heavyweight, and someday he wanted to be the heavyweight champion. He asked Martin about his chances of becoming a heavyweight; Martin looked at the 112-pound fighter and just shook his head in amazement. But Stoner had a different reaction. He told

Early in the history of professional boxing, contestants fought without the aid of protective gloves. These two men demonstrate the typical stance of bare-knuckled fighters.

Clay that he had the raw skill to become a champion—perhaps not the heavyweight champion but nonetheless a champion in whatever weight division he would naturally belong to once he matured.

However, Clay first had to perfect his boxing technique, Stoner said. He needed to stop flailing about; he should concentrate on conserving his energy by throwing fewer but more accurate punches. Encouraged by the confidence Stoner expressed in his ability, Clay, under Stoner's guidance, began honing the techniques he would use throughout the rest of his career: He improved the quickness of his punches; he began to fight more defensively, moving and circling around in the ring to avoid his opponent; and, in what would eventually become his trademark, he learned the art of leaning back, throwing a quick jab, then simply bending or leaning backward so that his opponent would miss on the counterpunch.

By 1958, Clay had improved his skills so much that he was able to win a berth in his first national Golden Gloves tournament, held in Chicago, Illinois. He had grown in size, too. At the age of 16, he had become a light heavyweight, weighing in at around 180 pounds. He did well in the tournament and won enough fights to make it past the semifinals, but he lost to another fighter in the final elimination round.

Dejected after his loss, Clay made his way back to the locker room. He was looking to have a conversation with some heavyweights to help take his mind off the defeat. He had the time to meet a few of them before he returned to Louisville.

In the locker room, Clay saw the Reverend Mr. Williams, a trainer from St. Louis, Missouri, whom he had met earlier in the week. He had developed a liking for the trainer partly because he managed only heavyweights. The Reverend Mr. Williams called them dinosaurs: They were so powerfully focused on their goals that they were always in danger of forgetting to

In 1908, Jack Johnson (shown here) became the first black world heavyweight champion. Two years later, he knocked out Jim Jeffries, a former champion who had been brought out of retirement by racist whites looking for a "white hope" to regain the title.

Ali won the light-heavyweight Golden Gloves national title in 1959 and 1960. He is shown here working out with fighter Jimmy Ellis (left) and trainer Joe Martin (right) during his preparation for the 1960 Golden Gloves tournament.

think of anything but their opponents. According to the Reverend Mr. Williams, heavyweights were lumbering predators who were so highly attuned to devouring other dinosaurs that they were as feared as the *Tyrannosaurus rex*. However, like the king of the dinosaurs, their narrow focus always put them in danger of extinction.

Clay went over to the reverend to ask him where he could find some heavyweights. He had noticed the flyweights and the lightweights chattering to each other all week long, but the heavyweights had kept mostly to themselves.

The reverend was taping the hands of one of his fighters in preparation for a bout. His answer to Clay's request to meet some heavyweights was direct. "Heavyweights don't hibernate together," the reverend said.

Clay asked him what he meant by not hibernating together.

"Run together, hide out together, buddy together," the Reverend Mr. Williams said. "Dinosaurs don't do that."

But why not? Clay wanted to know.

"It's against the law of nature," the reverend said. "Everybody got buddies, I know. But not dinosaurs. The dinosaur is different. He's got his own satellite. His own crowd."

"Birds of a different feather flock together," Clay insisted.

"But birds of prey don't flock together. And dinosaurs are demons of prey," the reverend said, having the last word.

Clay did not say anything in response; he was beginning to learn a few things about heavyweights.

He returned to the Golden Gloves national tournament again in 1959 and 1960, winning the light-heavyweight championship both times. In 1960, he also won the Amateur Athletic Union championship and qualified as a light heavyweight for the U.S.

Olympic boxing team. After another fighter distracted him by chattering in the ring during an Olympic trial bout, Clay picked up the habit, and it soon became one of his trademarks.

The 1960 Olympic Games were held in Rome, Italy—a fitting site for a young gladiator like Clay. Eighteen years old and very quick in and out of the ring, he was ready to show off his talent to the world. He advanced smoothly through the competition, and his talents were touted by the American television networks. For the first time in his career, millions of people in his own country and in other countries around the world got a good look at him. He was no longer a shy, awkward boy but a good-looking, likable, and talkative young man.

The championship bout in the 1960 Olympics was fought on September 5. Clay's opponent was a 23-year-old southpaw from Poland named Zbigniew Pietrzyskowski, a veteran of 230 fights. Clay had trouble at first against the more experienced left-handed fighter, but the young American gradually took con-

A determined Ali beats light-heavyweight Jimmy Jones (left) on March 10, 1960, to win the Golden Gloves national title.

Ali began to develop a worldwide following after winning a gold medal for boxing at the 1960 Olympic Games in Rome, Italy. He is shown here wearing his U.S. Olympic team jacket.

trol of the fight. He ended the bout by giving the Pole a tremendous battering in the last round, opening up a cut over Pietrzyskowski's left eye that made him vulnerable to Clay's right hook. The judges awarded Clay a unanimous 5–0 decision, which gave him the Olympic gold medal and the invaluable publicity that came with it.

Following his victory, Clay was at the top of the amateur boxing world. The next step for him was to become a professional boxer. Accordingly, serious courting by those who wanted to be his manager soon began.

One of the most important decisions that every fighter has to make is whom to choose as the person or organization that will represent him in the business of boxing. The manager's role is crucial because he is the person who books opponents, chooses venues, and negotiates contracts with clubs and coliseums as well as radio and television networks. For making the decisions that guide a fighter's career, the manager receives a portion of the boxer's fee for a fight. Under the best of circumstances, the manager consults with the boxer about these decisions so that there is agreement between them. However, many managers have tried to trick or bully a fighter—especially a young fighter—into signing unfair contracts or making other exploitative arrangements.

In the 1940s and 1950s, much of the fight business fell under the influence of organized crime. During that time, it was not unusual for a manager to demand that a fighter deliberately lose a match so that the racketeers could win large amounts of money by betting against the fighter. This type of match was known as a "fixed" fight, and it was only one of many ways that a manager who had made some sort of an arrangement with the criminal element could exploit a boxer. Because Clay was well aware of the pitfalls one could encounter when choosing a manager, he proceeded cautiously with his decision.

In the spring and summer before his Olympic victory, Clay had been approached through Martin by a wealthy Louisville businessman named William Reynolds, who was an heir to the Reynolds Aluminum fortune. Reynolds had heard that Clay was a major contender for the Olympic gold medal, and he was interested in backing Clay—by becoming his manager—once he became a professional fighter. Because Reynolds was already rich, it is probable that his interest in Clay had as much to do with the prestige of backing a champion fighter as it did with accumulating more money.

Reynolds sought to entice Clay by employing him as a laborer around his luxurious Louisville home. He also bought Clay new equipment and promised him a large contract if he won the gold medal. Yet Reynolds never gave Clay the feeling that he cared for him as a person. It seemed to Clay that Reynolds wanted to own him as though he were a piece of property, and this was not the kind of relationship that the young fighter wanted. He was too aware of his people's history of slavery to allow any manager to feel as though he owned him.

Immediately after Clay won the gold medal in Rome, Reynolds lavished attention on the new champion. On Clay's way back to Louisville from Italy, Reynolds let him stay free of charge for a week at his suite in New York City's luxurious Waldorf-Astoria Hotel. He provided Clay with money to buy expensive presents for his parents, and he provided him with pocket money to spend around town.

One of the first things that Clay did with Reynolds's money was to look up Sugar Ray Robinson, who had recently retired from the ring and was running a nightclub in Harlem. The former welterweight and middleweight champion had been one of Clay's heroes for some time. The young champion introduced himself to the old pro and then asked him to be his manager. Robinson, apparently content with

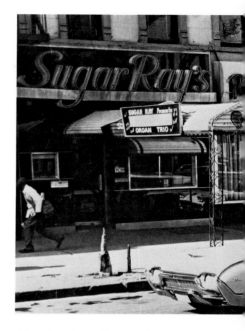

After the 1960 Olympic Games were over, Ali visited former boxing champion Sugar Ray Robinson at his nightclub in Harlem (shown here) intending to ask Robinson to serve as his manager.

his life and only dimly aware of who Clay was, turned down the young Olympian's offer.

Shortly after this encounter, Clay returned home to a hero's welcome in Louisville. He was feted and saluted by the governor of Kentucky as well as by both the mayor and the police chief of Louisville. He was even given a parade down the main street of his hometown. However, when he went to eat at a restaurant, he was refused service because he was black. He subsequently threw his Olympic gold medal into the Ohio River in disgust at the country he had represented at the Olympic Games.

Before long, Reynolds sent over his contract offer to manage Clay. So did former boxing champions Archie Moore and Rocky Marciano, the well-respected manager Cus D'Amato, and a group of 10 Louisville businessmen who called themselves the Louisville Millionaires. Clay and his father, with the

Ali (seated in center) signs a contract on October 27, 1960, calling for the Louisville Millionaires to serve as his managers for the next six years. His father looks on at the far left.

assistance of a trusted family attorney, looked over all of the offers carefully. The two best offers were from Reynolds and the Louisville Millionaires.

There was scarcely any difference between the two contracts, but Clay had little difficulty in deciding which one to accept. He informed an angry Martin that he was turning down Reynolds's offer. This rejection ended Clay's relationship not only with Reynolds but with Martin, too.

The Louisville Millionaires were headed by Bill Faversham, the son of an English actor. Their contract with Clay ran for six years, from 1960 to 1966. They gave him a $10,000 advance, and in turn they were to receive 50 percent of his earnings—both in and out of the ring—for the duration of their agreement. At the time, Clay felt lucky to have negotiated such a deal. He used the advance to pay off the mortgage of his parents' house and to repair its leaks and sagging porch. He also had the comfort of knowing that his managers were honest. They would stick to the agreement that the two parties had made; they would never ask him to deliberately lose a fight; and they would schedule him fairly, asking him to fight against equal and worthy opponents.

Next, Clay had to select the best trainer that he could find. Stoner had been a fine trainer for Clay when he was still an amateur. However, Stoner did not have the ring experience that the fighter needed now that he had become a professional.

The Louisville group knew that Archie Moore ran a boxing camp in the hills above San Diego in southern California. Moore had the experience that Clay was looking for: He had been actively involved in boxing since 1938, and he had won the light-heavyweight championship in 1952, keeping the title for 10 years. However, by 1960, Moore was 47 years old and nearing the end of his boxing career. He agreed to become Clay's trainer.

Moore's camp was in the country because he liked to isolate his fighters from distractions and temptations. He also felt that it was best to bring Clay along slowly toward the championship. Consequently, the young fighter was not allowed to spar with Moore himself until weeks after he had reported to the camp. Clay bridled at Moore's slow pace; he felt that he was ready to begin his climb to the top of the boxing world right away, and he pushed for a sparring session with the older fighter. (Sparring is when two boxers get into the ring to fight a practice round. Sparring rounds are usually three minutes long—the same length as a round in a regular boxing match. However, if a boxer wants to increase his stamina, he will spar for longer periods—sometimes up to seven or eight minutes a round.)

Clay finally succeeded in getting Moore into the ring with him, and the two fighters sparred for several rounds. Clay punched Moore all over the ring. He hit him with hooks, crosses, and uppercuts and generally took out his frustrations on Moore. After these rounds, Clay knew that he needed another trainer. Seeing how easily he handled the current light-heavyweight champion even if he was no longer in his prime convinced Clay that he was indeed ready to move ahead at a faster pace than Moore had suggested.

During the time that Clay spent in Moore's camp, he also learned that he could not train in isolation. He said:

> I decided that if I was going to be a fighter, I would have to train around people. I'd have to be around women and children, near barbershops, see people getting their shoes shined, watch the traffic, watch people go in and out of stores, hear them talk and talk back to them. And above all, I wanted to be associated with the instructor who would use his instructions on someone else. Not me. I had gone far past the training period. I wanted to fight, only to fight.

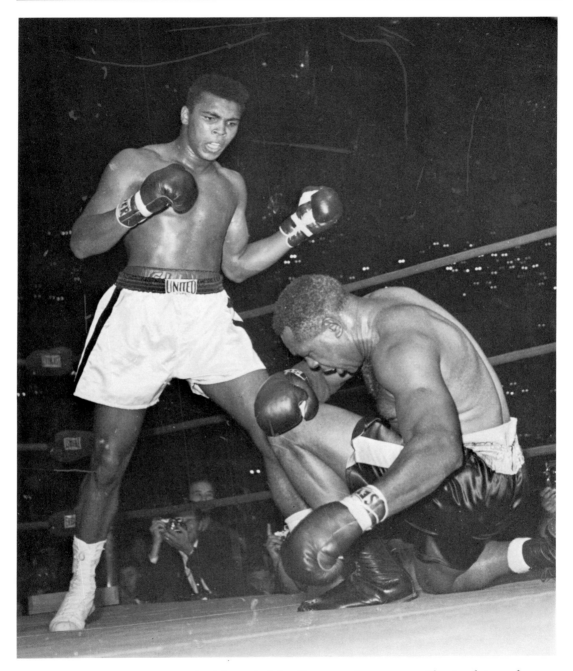

Former heavyweight champion Archie Moore (right) collapses on the canvas as Ali wins their confrontation on November 15, 1962, in four rounds—as he had predicted.

A full-blown heavyweight, Clay had indisputably become a dinosaur.

After leaving Moore's camp, Clay hooked up with a well-known trainer named Angelo Dundee, who had trained such top fighters as Carmen Basilio, Luis Rodriguez, and Willie Pastrano. Dundee knew how good Clay was, and he quickly agreed to take on the young contender. The trainer said of Clay, "He was always the first in and the last out of the gym."

With Dundee serving as his sounding board, Clay threw himself into the grinding tour of boxing that is typical of a hustling young professional. His first professional bout took place in Louisville on October 29, 1960. The result was a six-round decision over Tunney Hunsaker.

Clay fought eight bouts in 1961 and six in 1962, averaging a fight every seven weeks. He won all 14 of these fights, 12 of them by knockouts. In 1962, he also appeared in a minor role in the film version of Rod Serling's play *Requiem for a Heavyweight.*

One of the most interesting fights during this period in Clay's career was his match with Moore, his former trainer, in November 1962. Because they had once had a sparring session, the fight was, in a sense, a rematch. It was also Clay's first public match with a major fighter. The fight was televised, and Clay's share, $45,000, was at the time by far his largest purse.

Because Clay had so easily dominated Moore two years before, when he was still a green young pro, he was confident that he would win the match. What made the fight even more significant to him was that the reigning heavyweight champion, Charles "Sonny" Liston, would be in the audience. As was becoming Clay's style, he composed a poem that predicted the outcome of the match. "They'll all fall in the round I call!" he maintained, and he said before the Moore fight:

When you come to the fight,
Don't block the halls,
And don't block the door,
For y'all may go home,
After round four.

The fight was held on the older fighter's home ground, in Los Angeles, California, and the crowd was wildly partisan. In spite of the fans, who were screaming to Moore, "Shut him up," and, "Hit him in the mouth," Clay methodically demolished his opponent in four rounds, just as he had predicted in his poem.

An intriguing encounter occurred in Clay's dressing room after the fight. Amid the laughter and joking of Clay's entourage, Liston walked into the room to meet the new contender. Clay looked at his chief rival, who was known for his ice-cold stare, and proclaimed:

King Liston will stay,
Only until he meets Cassius Clay.
Moore fell in four,
Liston in eight.

Liston just glared at Clay. The reigning champion then said, "You go eight seconds with me, little boy, and I'll give you the title."

After concluding a workout, Ali composes a poem predicting the outcome of his next fight. His brief rhymes were designed to amuse his fans and destroy his opponents' confidence.

4

A CALL
FROM
ISLAM

ᘓᘐᘓ

Ali joined the Nation of Islam, a black-separatist religious group, in the early 1960s. He is shown here speaking at a meeting attended by Elijah Muhammad (right), who founded the group.

URING CLAY'S NEXT three fights in 1963, he strove to perfect the antics that would make him stand out in the crowded field of heavyweight contenders. While he continued to predict, with his own style of poetry, the round in which he would knock out his opponent, he also performed some new publicity stunts. Traveling outside the United States for the first time as a professional, he went to England to fight the British heavyweight champion, Henry Cooper. Before the fight, Clay donned a crown and cape and declared himself "the uncrowned king of heavyweights." He also predicted that he would knock out Cooper in the fifth round. The English fans flocked to see Clay get his comeuppance, only to watch Cooper fall in the sixth round.

Clay's campaign to seek recognition for himself worked. The more he bragged, strutted, and spouted his poetry, the more he stirred up the boxing world—and an aroused boxing world always means more money for a boxer. This was one of the main reasons for Clay's theatrics.

After the Cooper fight, Jack Nilon, Liston's manager, stopped by Clay's dressing room with the news that Liston had decided to fight Clay. Nilon also said that he had a message to deliver from the champion to Clay: He should "drink [his] orange juice and milk shakes" and "stay well for the fight." However, Clay, who had recently married Sonji Roi, should not stay up late worrying about the outcome of the money-making fight because, according to Liston, "now your wife can be a rich widow." The match was set for February 25, 1964, in Miami, Florida.

Liston's offer to fight Clay was proof that the young challenger had gained enough notoriety for himself to grab the champion's undivided attention. In the months before his fight with Cooper in England, Clay had stalked Liston across the United States. In Las Vegas, Nevada, shortly before Liston was scheduled to fight Floyd Patterson, Clay had disrupted a blackjack game in which Liston was playing by yelling that he, Clay, was the real champ—the man who would put Liston to the ultimate test. Liston, having been tipped off about Clay, then pulled a pistol from his jacket and fired it several times in Clay's direction, which sent Clay running for his life through the casino hall. Even Clay was amused when he found out later that the shots had been blanks.

A few weeks after the showdown in the casino, Clay again tweaked the champion by showing up outside Liston's house in Denver, Colorado, early one morning, screaming how he wanted to "whip the champ" then and there in his front yard. Liston came out of his house, and the police arrived just as he was smashing in the windows of Clay's bus. The next day, many of the nation's major papers carried stories about the incident—as Clay had hoped they would.

Besides attracting publicity, Clay's antics also served another of the challenger's goals. They presumably made Liston wonder about Clay's sanity. Clay felt that the champion might lose a bit of his confidence and concentration if he spent part of his time brooding about the mental health of his opponent. Sometimes all that a boxer needs to give himself an advantage in an important fight is to cause a minor lapse in his opponent's mental preparation.

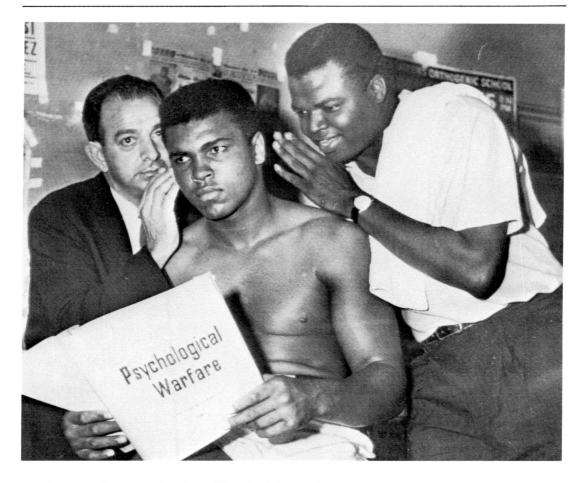

During the months that Clay had been dashing around the country, bewildering and intriguing people with his curious behavior, he had also quietly begun studying the precepts of the religion of Islam and meeting with representatives of a black American religious group called the Lost-Found Nation of Islam. Founded in 1931 by Elijah Muhammad, the group follows a philosophy that is largely based on the teachings of Muhammad, the 7th-century founder of the religion of Islam. However, the Nation of Islam also preaches the doctrine of independence and self-help for black Americans.

Ali perfects his tactics while preparing for his first meeting with heavyweight champion Charles "Sonny" Liston. The challenger is flanked here by his trainer, Angelo Dundee (left), and his second, Drew "Bundini" Brown (right).

In the early 1960s, the Nation of Islam advocated total separation of black and white Americans. The group, whose members are called Black Muslims, labeled whites as "devils" who were responsible for the plight of blacks all around the world. The Black Muslims suggested that the states of Mississippi and Alabama be partitioned off from the United States as an independent nation for blacks who were then living in America. The preachers of the Nation of Islam also insisted that members of their mosques drop their surnames, which they pointed out were not the original names of their ancestors from Africa but the names of slave owners, and adopt instead the letter X, which would stand for their lost African name or some appropriate Muslim name.

Thus, in the summer of 1963, Clay more or less secretly changed his name—first to Cassius X, then to Muhammad Ali. Publicly, he was still known as Cassius Clay. However, to his Black Muslim brothers and sisters, he was known as Muhammad Ali.

Ali subsequently hired several Muslims to join his entourage. He took on Captain Samuels, the leader of the Miami mosque of the Nation of Islam, as his security chief and bodyguard, and he retained the services of several Muslim women to cook the careful and restricted diet that is required of all followers of the Nation of Islam. He also forswore the use of alcohol, coffee, cigarettes, and all nonmedicinal drugs.

Ali had good reason to keep his conversion to Islam a secret: Racial tensions in America in the 1960s were reaching a breaking point. As members of civil rights groups pressed their demands for racial justice and equality in the South, their demands were officially met by attacks from the police and, unofficially, by violence from white racists; elsewhere, the black ghettos of most big cities were seething with tension.

The Nation of Islam was then one of the most radical of the black groups demanding change. Spurred

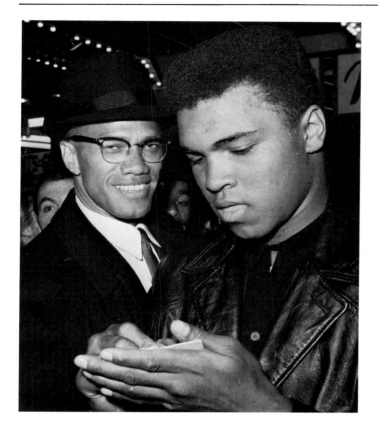

Ali confers with Malcolm X (left) shortly before the civil rights leader was suspended from the Black Muslim movement. When Malcolm X proceeded to form his own nationalist groups, Ali elected to remain with Elijah Muhammad and the Nation of Islam.

on by Malcolm X, who had become one of the group's most vigorous leaders, the Black Muslim movement was attracting an increasing number of converts in the major cities of America. It was also attracting much criticism for its views on race relations.

Three days before Ali's championship match with Liston, Bill McDonald, the promoter of the fight, learned of Ali's association with the Black Muslims. Malcolm X had visited Ali's gym in Miami, and newspapers in New York had carried articles about Ali's visit to a Muslim mosque in Harlem. Claiming that Ali's conversion to Islam was bad publicity for the fight and could cause him to lose the money he had invested in promoting the fight, McDonald demanded that Ali make a public statement disavowing support for the Nation of Islam. Ali refused to do this, so McDonald tried to cancel the fight. A day of tense confrontations between the white promoter and the black challenger followed. The reluctant promoter was persuaded to let the fight go on only after hours of wrangling with Ali's trainer, Angelo Dundee, and his managers, the Louisville Millionaires.

As the time for Ali's first heavyweight championship bout drew closer, he had another problem to worry about in addition to McDonald's threat to cancel the fight. He had begun to receive threatening phone calls from people who had learned of his conversion to Islam and disapproved of his outrageous behavior. Racial slurs and death threats were hurled at him. He was told that no matter what he might do in the ring, he would not win the fight.

Ali became extremely cautious, even with those who were helping him train. He knew that two ways to defeat a boxer were to poison the water he drank between rounds and to put an astringent substance that would affect his vision into the water that was used to wipe his face between rounds. Consequently, Ali allowed only Muslims to handle these chores; even Angelo Dundee, who would remain with Ali throughout his career, was prohibited from doing them.

The title bout began with Ali, still known to most of the world as Cassius Clay, and Liston facing each other in the ring as the referee gave them instructions. Ali talked through his mouthpiece to Liston, who, as he usually did just before a fight was about to begin, silently stared at his opponent. A former union strongman, Liston was big and tough. His wrists were as large as most men's calves, and he was one of the hardest punchers in all of boxing.

Looking for a quick knockout, Liston charged Ali in the first round, relentlessly stalking him around the ring. Sometimes Liston even ran right at him to deliver his ferocious roundhouse punches, which Ali neatly sidestepped or avoided by using a trick he had discovered at Stoner's Louisville gym: He would lean away from an oncoming punch at the last possible moment, and the punch would harmlessly whiz by his face. Ali did not throw many punches until he had gauged Liston's strategy, which was to score a knockout as early as possible. In the latter part of the first round, Ali began to hit Liston with quick, precise jabs that snapped the champion's head around.

The second and third rounds continued in the same way, with Liston swinging wildly, trying for a knockout, and Ali dancing and darting around the ring, never getting hit hard while lacing Liston with jabs that began to dull the champion's reactions. Suddenly, near the end of the third round, Ali hit his opponent with a glancing shot to the head that opened a cut under Liston's left eye. Liston had never been cut before, and he began to panic once he realized what had happened to him.

By leaning back suddenly, Ali manages to stay clear of a powerful left hook by Sonny Liston (left) during their first meeting, on February 25, 1964. Ali had been practicing this maneuver since the start of his career.

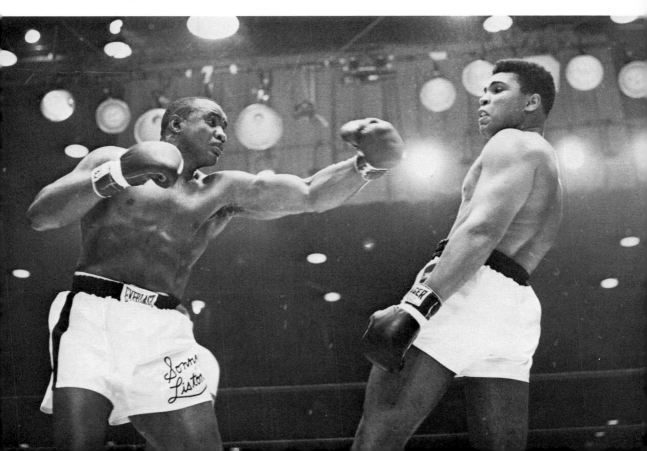

Liston was not used to going beyond three or four rounds; in most of his fights, he had knocked out his opponent before the fifth round. As the fourth round took place, the champion began to tire. Knowing that his energy was waning and that the cut under his eye, which had been treated between rounds, could be reopened at any time, he desperately continued to press his assault against Ali. But Ali was maddeningly difficult to catch and hit. He danced and circled around Liston and started talking to the older man more and more, taunting him.

During the fourth round, Liston pulled a muscle in his shoulder while throwing a desperation punch at Ali. When the round was over, Liston's trainer rubbed the fighter's shoulder with liniment to keep

Ali is named heavyweight champion of the world: Raising his arms in triumph at the announcement of his victory over Sonny Liston on February 25, 1964, Ali receives a hug from Drew "Bundini" Brown as Angelo Dundee runs joyously to greet them in the center of the ring.

the muscle from tightening up. The medication got into Ali's eyes in the fifth round as the two fighters clinched. Fearing that Liston's gloves had been doctored with the liniment, Ali stumbled around the ring, literally holding off Liston at arm's length. When Ali returned to his corner at the end of the fifth round, he insisted that Dundee stop the fight and have Liston's gloves examined. Instead of stopping the fight, the shrewd Dundee calmed down his fighter. He told Ali that he had come too far to stop now; he must get back into the ring and beat Liston.

Ali's eyesight slowly cleared up in the sixth round. However, Liston was still having his troubles. He was breathing heavily; his energy was spent. And he could not punch well with his damaged arm. Ali hit him with some more hard shots to the head before the round ended. He was giving substance to the slogan that Drew "Bundini" Brown had recently come up with for Ali: "Float like a butterfly, sting like a bee."

When the bell rang for the start of the seventh round, an astonishing thing happened: Liston sat sulking on his stool in his corner; he would not come into the ring. The fight was over! Ali saw his trainers and cornermen throw up their hands and heard them shout with joy as they rushed into the ring. Then he heard an announcement that was similar to those sweet words that he remembered coming from a car radio on the streets of Louisville: "Ladies and gentlemen, the new heavyweight champion of the world . . ."

The day after the fight, Ali publicly announced his conversion to Islam and the change in his name. The new champion then took some time off from boxing. He visited Africa and the Middle East, and he began granting interviews to the major papers of the world and making appearances on American television. Many who were not boxing fans soon grew familiar with Ali.

Drew "Bundini" Brown (left) escorts an emotionally drained Ali to his dressing room moments after he has scored a technical knockout over Sonny Liston for his first heavyweight title.

Ali went on a tour of Africa and the Middle East shortly after he became the heavyweight champion of the world in 1964. He is shown here dressed in a traditional African costume, being greeted by a group of cheering youngsters in Nigeria.

It was not too long before Ali returned to the ring—the ring was not only his paycheck; it was his life as well. Besides his need to box, he craved the adulation of his fans and the exaltation that came with fame and success. A rematch with Liston was scheduled for May 25, 1965, in Lewiston, Maine.

Ali's personal triumph was diminished somewhat by several events that took place between the first and second fights with Liston. In 1964, shortly after Ali won the heavyweight title, Malcolm X broke rank with the Nation of Islam and formed his own religious and political groups dedicated to spiritual enlightenment and social justice. A feud quickly developed between the followers of Elijah Muhammad and those who left the Nation of Islam to join Malcolm X. Ali chose to remain loyal to the Nation of Islam even though he admired Malcolm X.

In February 1965, Malcolm X was assassinated in New York City. Two of those charged with his murder were Black Muslims from the New York mosque of the Nation of Islam. As Ali trained for his rematch with Liston, he not only received the usual threatening calls from white racists; he also received death threats from people who claimed to be followers of Malcolm X. Ali was subsequently guarded by the FBI and the local police during the month and a half that preceded the fight.

Just as Ali was facing danger due to his religious life, his personal life grew troubled as well: His marriage to Sonji was beginning to come apart. Because his wife was not interested in Islam, she refused to stop smoking and wearing makeup. Nor did she want to wear the austere clothing that women are required to wear by the Nation of Islam. The night before his fight with Liston, Ali and Sonji agreed to get a divorce.

Because of these crises and distractions, Ali's concentration was not totally focused on his opponent when he stepped into the ring to fight Liston for the

A prominent member of the Black Muslims, Ali became the target of death threats in 1965, shortly after the assassination of Malcolm X. The heavyweight champion is shown here on his way to a religious meeting in New York surrounded by some of his bodyguards.

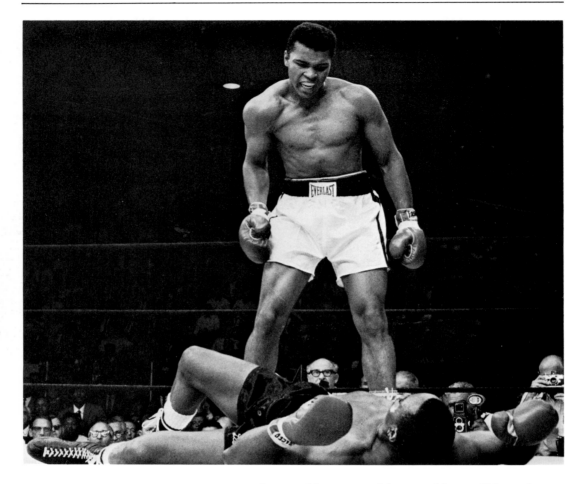

Ali tells Sonny Liston to get up during the first round of their heavyweight championship rematch on May 25, 1965. However, Liston failed to rise from the canvas after being hit by a punch that was reportedly not strong enough "to crush a grape."

second time. However, Ali spared himself from facing a long and punishing fight, which he might have lost. In the first round, he hit Liston with what looked like a weak punch, and the man whom Ali had labeled "the big, ugly bear" crumpled to the mat. He stayed down for the count; when he finally got up, he appeared more than a little bit dazed. Ali had beaten Liston for the second—and last—time.

Many sportswriters were uncertain about exactly what took place during the fight. It seemed to them that Ali had finished off Liston too quickly, too easily. Suspicions circulated that the fight had been fixed. However, tape replays of the fight show that Liston was hit solidly by a fast punch. Just how hard the punch was and how hard it jarred him, no one but Liston can say.

Ali had only one more fight in 1965, with former heavyweight champion Floyd Patterson, a gutsy fighter whose personality was the opposite of Ali's. Whereas Ali was loud and extravagant, Patterson was quiet and dignified. Ali, after refusing to renounce the Nation of Islam, had become one of America's most visible symbols of black pride. Patterson was not a leading figure in the struggle for racial equality (although he was clearly involved in the struggle). However, the mainstream press, which was controlled mostly by whites, was cheering for Patterson to take the title away from Ali. Reacting to their favoritism, Ali labeled Patterson as a "black white hope," alluding to the days in the early 1900s when a number of white fighters tried to take away the heavyweight title from Jack Johnson, the first black world champion. On November 11 in Las Vegas, Patterson fought bravely for 12 rounds until Ali battered him into submission.

In 1966, Ali's contract with the Louisville Millionaires expired, and he took on a new manager, Herbert Muhammad, the son of the founder of the Nation of Islam, Elijah Muhammad. Ali's earnings rose significantly with Herbert Muhammad as his manager. In his first three fights under Muhammad, Ali earned an average of $420,000 per fight—much more than he had been making with his former managers.

In the two years that followed the Patterson fight, Ali fought every major heavyweight contender and beat all of them, mostly by knockouts. By 1967, he had virtually run out of opponents. He was in peak form. Nothing, it seemed, could stop Ali from becoming the greatest heavyweight champion of all time. **(S)**

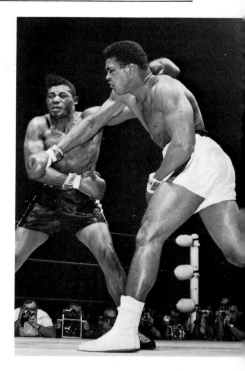

Ali hits Floyd Patterson (left) with a right to the jaw during their heavyweight championship fight on November 11, 1965. Ali won the fight against the former heavyweight titleholder in 12 rounds.

A TECHNICAL KNOCKOUT

—————— ❧ ——————

J UST WHEN THE goals that Ali had worked so hard for had been reached and his life seemed to be in almost perfect order, unforeseen events conspired to shatter his sense of harmony and success. His initial confrontation with such trouble came in 1964, in the form of a notice from the U.S. Selective Service Board, which he received just before his first fight with Liston. The young fighter ignored the notice that he was to attend an entrance examination for the army. Ali, who was then 22 years old, had been obtaining postponements of this examination since his 18th birthday. These postponements had been arranged by his influential managers, the Louisville Millionaires, who had wanted to see him make as much money as he could before his induction into the army.

The summons from the Selective Service Board ordered Ali to appear at the board's office in Miami so that his draft status could be judged by the board's officials. Beginning in the early 1950s, the United States manned its armed forces by means of a system called the universal military draft. According to this system, all young men were required by law to join a branch of the armed forces soon after their 18th birthday or graduation from high school. Under cer-

Ali talks to reporters outside the federal courthouse in Houston, Texas, on April 28, 1967, after announcing his refusal to be inducted into the army.

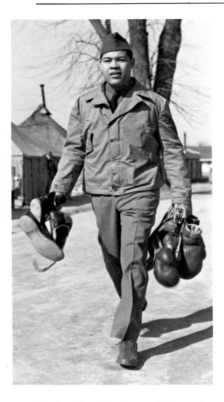

Rather than having to fight on the battlefield during his stint in the army, undefeated heavyweight champion Joe Louis (shown here) was asked to boost the morale of American troops at home and abroad during World War II.

tain circumstances, a young man such as Ali could delay his entrance into the army for a few years. However, the draft was a federal institution that every young American male had to reckon with sooner or later.

The draft was made "universal" so that the burden of defending the country would be shared equally by all ethnic, religious, and social groups. At least this was how the system was ideally supposed to work. In reality, many people were exempted from the draft: those who were mentally, emotionally, or physically incapable of service; those with families to support; and those who were studying at a college or a university.

The summons from the Selective Service Board was particularly worrisome to Ali because his induction into the army would disrupt his professional career for at least two years. Other well-known fighters had been called to serve in the armed forces before Ali. The most notable example was the heavyweight champion Joe Louis, who served in the army during World War II. As a celebrated boxer, Louis served a ceremonial tour of duty. He was not sent to the battlefront; instead, he was asked to visit bases and hospitals both in the United States and abroad.

Ali knew that he would be drafted sooner or later because he did not qualify for an exemption from the draft; although he had a wife to support, the large amounts of money he had been making disqualified him from obtaining an exemption so he could provide for his family. Yet he had been given assurances that when he was eventually drafted into the army, he would not be sent to Vietnam as a combat soldier. Instead, his stint would be along the lines of Louis's. After all, Ali, too, was a celebrated boxer.

However, Ali's conscience and his Muslim beliefs were causing him to consider refusing induction into the army because he was politically and morally op-

posed to America's increasing involvement in the
Vietnam War. As a member of the Nation of Islam,
he believed (with a few exceptions) that the taking
of life in warfare was not morally justifiable. He also
believed that the government and the people of the
United States should not be involved in what Elijah
Muhammad called "a fight inside the Vietnamese's
own family."

The members of the Nation of Islam also felt that
black Americans were "subject peoples" within their
own country. Consequently, they should not be asked
to fight another non-Caucasian group—in this case,
the Vietnamese. Believing that the Vietnam War
marked the domination of a foreign race by the white
American ruling class, the Black Muslims maintained
that such a fight was the responsibility of whites only.

Ali and the Nation of Islam were not alone in
holding these views. By 1964, many young Americans from all different racial backgrounds strongly
disagreed with the their country's policy in Southeast
Asia—and many of them, like Ali, were willing to
express their disagreement by refusing induction into
the army. In doing so, they risked a prison sentence
of five years or the possibility of a long exile if they
chose to avoid the draft by leaving the country.

Ali's refusal to participate in the Vietnam War drew the support of many young Americans, whose demands for an end to U.S. involvement in Southeast Asia increased dramatically as the war escalated in the late 1960s.

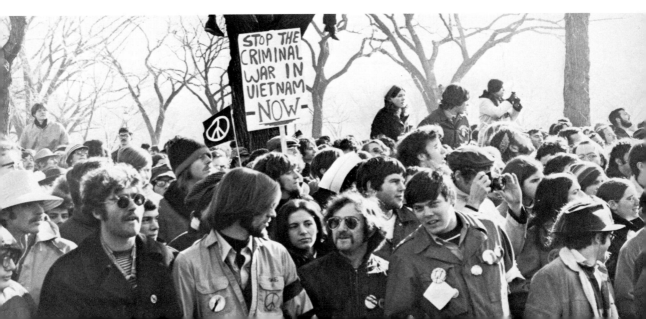

Ali eventually flunked the intelligence test of the Selective Service examination because he did not answer a number of the questions. He claimed that he had left some of the responses blank because he did not know the answers to the questions and was reluctant to risk a guess. Others thought differently of his actions, which resulted in his receiving a temporary deferment from the army. Congressman Mendel Rivers of South Carolina stated:

Clay's deferment is an insult to every mother's son serving in Vietnam. Here he is, smart enough to finish high school, write his kind of poetry, promote himself all over the world, make a million a year, drive around in red Cadillacs—and they say he's too dumb to tote a gun. Who's dumb enough to believe that?

During Ali's attempt to avoid induction into the army, he won the support of civil rights leader Martin Luther King, Jr. (third from right).

Such an outcry not only showed the congressman's contempt for Ali but indicated little appreciation for the feeling of resentment against the war that was growing throughout the United States.

In fact, the antiwar movement represented just one of many great changes that were sweeping the nation in the 1960s. The civil rights movement, which attacked racism through large-scale demonstrations, changed forever the relations between black and white Americans. America's youth, quiet and conformist through the 1950s, suddenly became noisy and critical of the flaws in American society and culture in the 1960s. Rock and roll became the music of youthful protest and celebration. The birth control pill, widely available for the first time in the early 1960s, heralded a new era of sexual freedom. Old and established moral certainties were being challenged everywhere. Yet it was the Vietnam War more than anything else that symbolized to a generation of rebellious Americans what had gone wrong with their country.

By 1967, Americans no longer saw the conflict in Vietnam as a minor skirmish at the edge of the civilized world. The U.S. government was spending $2 billion a month on the war and had 450,000 troops stationed in Vietnam. Every week almost 100 American soldiers died fighting in Vietnam and more than 500 were wounded. And most crucial to the making of public opinion, this drama of human suffering was broadcast every night via television into the homes of millions of Americans.

Mass resistance against an unpopular war was not an entirely new phenomenon in American history; it had occurred at the beginning of the Civil War nearly a century before. However, resistance to a war and refusal of induction on such a large scale was new to 20th-century America, and it caused resentment and bitterness between three generations of Americans: On one side of this conflict were the

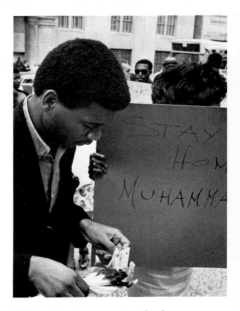

While Ali announces inside the federal courthouse in Houston, Texas, that he is refusing induction into the army, an antiwar demonstrator (shown here) burns his military draft card outside the building. Burning one's draft card was a popular act of defiance by those who refused to fight in the Vietnam War.

While Ali was protesting against an unpopular war, he remained a favorite sports figure to most of the American public. Children found his playful nature to be especially appealing.

veterans of World War I and those who had willingly fought in World War II, and on the other side were their sons and grandsons, who did not want to fight the Vietcong in Vietnam.

Although Ali was caught in the middle of this conflict, his life in the mid-1960s was not entirely filled with confrontation. He loved the camera, and the camera treated him favorably in return. People around the world responded warmly to his sincerity and to his obvious love of children, even if at times they were baffled by his wilder antics.

To many in America, Ali seemed to be a new kind of black man—one who either delighted or horrified his audience, depending on their beliefs and cultural background. He was utterly confident (even cocky), articulate, assertive, and in turn playful and serious. And he was always challenging conventional wisdom and authority. With the possible exception of the Brazilian soccer star Pelé, he was the most popular sports figure on earth in the mid-1960s.

By 1967, Ali had been the undisputed heavyweight champion for three years, and he had gone beyond the confines of boxing to become a media celebrity. His words and deeds had been denounced and encouraged, explained and analyzed, in every major language of the world. Every other week, it seemed, he had a new prediction in verse about the state of the world or the fate of his next opponent in the ring.

Ali loved his star status and went out of his way to stir up controversy. He courted other celebrities and notable figures—persons as diverse as the popular wrestler Gorgeous George and the British mathematician and philosopher Bertrand Russell. However, Ali's media whirligigs always had a point: They drew people to his fights and increased his purse—the money he could demand for his performance in the ring.

In many ways, Ali was a creature of his age. At a time when the influential artistic movement known

as pop (which was short for "popular") art was com-
bining high and low culture, the comical and the
serious, so was Ali. A clear example of his "pop"
sensibility took place on a television talk show in
1965. Ali spoke about his upcoming fight with Patterson, then read some of his poetry while the flamboyant entertainer Liberace played a piano in the
background. Ali's poetry began:

> It all started twenty years past,
> The Greatest of them All was born at last.
> The very first words from his Louisville lips
> "I'm pretty as a picture and there's no one I can't whip."

Although Ali often displayed his comic side to
the public, he could also be quite serious about his
beliefs and very stubborn in defending them. As
America's involvement in Vietnam wore on, Ali
needed these qualities to face the difficult times that
lay ahead.

Until 1966, Ali's status in the files of the Selective
Service Board remained classified as 1-Y, the des-
ignation given to those who had failed either the
physical or written part of the Selective Service
examination. However, in February 1966, new reg-
ulations lowered the requirements of the army draft.
This caused Ali's hometown draft board to change
his status to 1-A, making him a suitable candidate
for service in the armed forces.

Ali was informed of the change in his draft status
while he was in training for the third defense of his
title. He responded with a stanza of impromptu poetry:

> Keep asking me, no matter how long
> On the war in Vietnam, I sing this song
> I ain't got no quarrel with the Viet Cong . . .

This bit of doggerel, broadcast that very evening
on television news programs around the country, kicked
up a storm of controversy and led eventually to Ali's

being banned from the profession of boxing. The first state of note that prohibited him from boxing was Illinois. Before his remark about the Vietcong, Ali had been scheduled to defend his title in Chicago against Ernie Terrell. Yet several weeks after Ali recited the Vietcong poem, the Illinois Boxing Commission demanded that he come before them to disavow what he had said. Ali appeared before the commission, but he would not apologize. The commission then refused him the right to fight in Illinois. The Terrell fight was canceled (it was later held in Houston, on February 6, 1967), and Ali in 1966 was forced to schedule all of his fights but one in foreign cities: He fought and beat George Chuvalo in Toronto, Canada, Henry Cooper and Brian London in London, England, and Karl Mildenberger in Frankfurt, West Germany; he defeated Cleveland Williams in Houston.

While this ban was taking place, Ali's lawyers changed the location of his draft board from Louisville to Houston in the hope that he would find more

Ernie Terrell (left) receives a savage beating from Ali during their heavyweight championship bout in Houston, Texas, on February 6, 1967. Originally scheduled to take place during the previous year in Chicago, Illinois, the match had to be relocated after the Illinois Boxing Commission refused to let Ali fight in the midwestern state.

sympathetic treatment in the Texas city. But this was not to happen. Ali, true to his word, refused induction inside the courthouse in Houston. For this act of defiance, he was found guilty by an all-white jury of draft evasion and was sentenced to a five-year jail term.

Ali's lawyer, Robert Arum, began to appeal the conviction through the court system; during this period of appeal, Ali remained free on bail. However, what had been started by the Illinois Boxing Commission continued throughout the country, until Ali was banned from fighting in every state. The state of New York, along with several other states, revoked his boxing license, and the World Boxing Association (WBA) stripped him of his world heavyweight championship title.

Unable to practice his profession, Ali found it difficult to earn a living. For a while, he was not even allowed to leave the country because the government had revoked his passport; the government insisted that he had to remain in the country until his court case was resolved. Ali was convinced that he had done the right thing and that someday the righteousness of his beliefs would prevail. But for the time being, he had no choice but to carry on while seeking strength and understanding in the words of his spiritual leader, Elijah Muhammad:

> Of this grief you and I must suffer, all these burdens we must bear. . . . I have no alternative than to tell you that there is not any life beyond the grave. There is no justice in the sweet bye and bye. Immortality is NOW, HERE. We are the blessed of God and we must exert every means to protect ourselves.

Ali did not know how long it would be before he was able to resume his boxing career. Yet throughout this period of his being banned, which he called "the Exile," he drew on the teachings of the Nation of Islam and never gave in to despair. ❧

Attorney Robert Arum (shown here) was employed by Ali to appeal the charges of draft evasion that had been filed by the U.S. government against the heavyweight champion. Winning this appeal helped to end Ali's banishment from professional boxing.

the fight in Atlanta. A note on one of the packages said only: "To Cassius Clay from Georgia." In one package was a dead black Chihuahua. In the other package was found a handmade doll that somewhat resembled Ali. A note next to the doll read: "We know how to handle black draft-dodging dogs in Georgia. Stay out of Atlanta." Ali buried the little dog; he kept the doll. It would inspire him to get ready for the fight.

Even though Ali's ribs were causing him much pain, he knew that he could not postpone the Quarry fight. To do so would risk the gains he had made thus far. Besides, even at half strength and with bruised ribs, he was confident that he could beat Quarry. He had fought Liston in their second fight with bruised ribs, although he had been lucky that the Liston rematch had lasted only one round. Still, Quarry was not in the same class as Liston.

Even if Ali was somewhat less than fully ready for Quarry, the public—as had been demonstrated at the exhibition—was ready for Ali. By the day of the fight, October 26, 1970, Atlanta's hotels were filled with a wide range of people—including many celebrities—who had come to the city to attend the fight. By the time of the match, the atmosphere surrounding the event resembled a convention for people whose dress and demeanor were extravagant and often outrageous: Men wore mink porkpie hats, tuxedos, and full-length fur coats; women had on diamonds and bright, glittery evening gowns.

The two boxers entered the arena. The referee read the rules to them; the boxers touched gloves with each other and returned to their corners. Then the bell rang, and the crowd was on its feet and yelling. Ali was finally back.

Quarry tried to take the fight to Ali in the first round. He came in close to Ali in an attempt to slug it out with the former champion. Ali was ready for

All sorts of celebrities and supporters—including the mink-clad fan shown here—added to the electrifying atmosphere that generally surrounded Ali on the night of a fight.

this tactic. Whenever Quarry charged him, he spun away from the approaching fighter and danced to the left, but not before landing a jab or a combination of hooks and jabs. The crowd was pleased. This was the familiar, dancing Ali, frustrating his opponent with his quick feet and hurting him with his fast hands.

Ali moved faster in the first round than he had in any fight since the Liston matches. It was quite a show by the 28-year-old grand master of boxing, and at the bell the crowd stood on its feet again to applaud him. The second round went much the same as the first: Quarry rushed Ali, who skipped around the ring and hit Quarry with a few lightning-quick combinations before retreating. By the end of the first two rounds, Quarry had hardly touched Ali.

Quarry slowed down a little in the third round, and in response, so did Ali. Still dancing, but attacking rather than retreating, he hit Quarry with some hard shots. Suddenly, a little over halfway through the round, he hit Quarry with a left hook that opened up a gash over Quarry's left eye. With the blood from the cut impairing Quarry's vision, Ali began to hit the wounded fighter with a furious volley of punches, pummeling him until the bell sounded the end of the third round.

Quarry's manager, seeing that the cut over his fighter's eye was too deep to patch up adequately, threw in the towel before the start of the fourth round, and the fight was stopped. Ali had won his 30th professional fight without a loss, and Quarry had been his 24th knockout victim.

Sportswriter Steve Cady of the *New York Times* hailed Ali as a "black prince, a folk hero who convinced white America that blacks really existed." Ali himself picked up this black-white theme in a later interview in which he expressed his emotions about the fight. He said, "When I climb into the ring, I'm

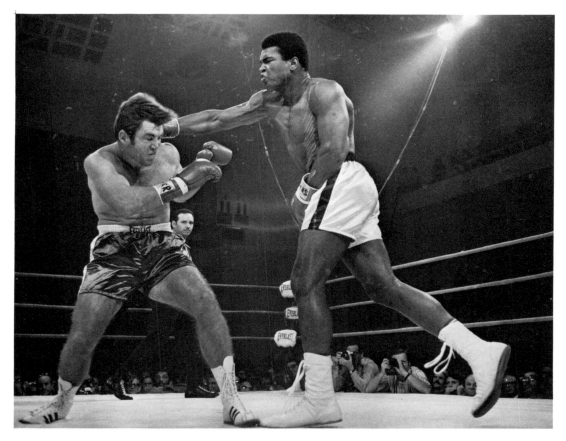

thinking about God, and I'm thinking about all those people in every ghetto in every city in the United States of America. I'm out to whip all the hypocrites of the power structure. I'm fighting for my freedom and carrying the hopes of my 30 million black people here."

Ali, hero or devil incarnate (depending on one's way of seeing things), was most definitely back in full form. It would be only a matter of time before Frazier was forced to take his measure. Ali had to fight only one more contender, the South American Oscar Bonavena, before Frazier finally agreed to confront him.

Shortly after Ali dispatched Bonavena with a knockout in the 15th round, he and Frazier set March

Hard rights by Ali—such as the one shown here—opened up a gash over the left eye of Jerry Quarry (left) and caused their fight on October 26, 1970, to be stopped after the third round.

Ali is presented with the Martin Luther King, Jr., Sports Medallion by civil rights leaders Coretta Scott King (center) and Ralph Abernathy (second from right) shortly after his victory over Jerry Quarry.

8, 1971, as the date for their historic showdown. The site was Ali's favorite haunt from earlier days, Madison Square Garden in New York City. Warming to his latest opponent, Ali predicted a sixth-round knockout of Frazier.

The fight is still regarded as one of the classic contests in boxing history. In many ways, it led to a new era in boxing. For the first time in history, a championship fight was viewed by a truly worldwide audience. Approximately 300 million people watched the match on closed-circuit television. Madison Square Garden broke all of its records by selling an amazing $1,350,000 worth of tickets for the privilege of viewing the fight live in the arena.

Frazier and his manager, Yank Durham, were as savvy a pair of strategists as existed in boxing. Yet their plan to beat Ali was brutally simple: Kill the body and the head will follow. This meant that Frazier was to pound Ali's stomach, ribs, chest, and back relentlessly—until Ali was in such pain that he would lose his concentration. Then Frazier would go for the knockout punch to the head.

The trouble with this strategy—as Durham and Frazier knew—was that many other boxers had tried to catch Ali before but none had succeeded. No one had ever come close to seriously hurting him. However, Frazier had proved that he could punch and that he could take a punch. He was built solidly, yet he was surprisingly quick for his size.

Dressed in street clothes, Ali steps into the ring with heavyweight champion Joe Frazier (right) before the start of an exhibition bout in 1971. Such antic showmanship at a rival's match was characteristic of Ali.

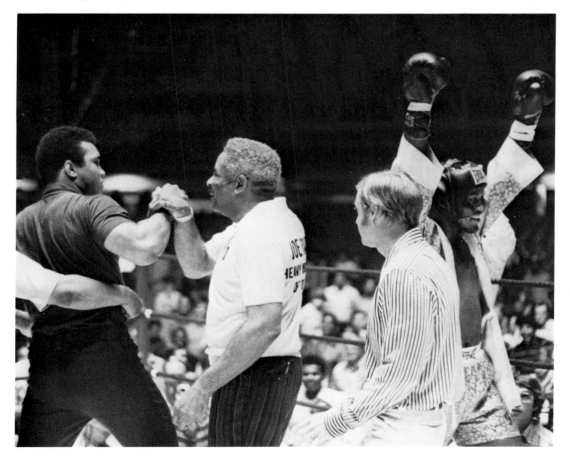

The fight began predictably enough. Like Quarry and many others, Frazier came right at Ali. But what Ali did was astonishing. Rather than dancing to avoid Frazier's rush, he positioned himself on the ropes, leaning into them and then bouncing off them, and fought Frazier straight on. Ali later nicknamed this tactic "rope-a-dope" to indicate that the opponent who had resolved to pound Ali's body while he protected himself on the ropes was a fool: For such an opponent would wear himself out by punching Ali's arms, gloves, and elbows; he would then be vulnerable to a comparatively fresher Ali several rounds later. Ali's presumption was that his opponent would eventually tire, at which point he could counterattack and try for a knockout.

Frazier's big punch—his knockout blow—was his left hook, which Ali avoided mainly by using his own left as the lead punch. If a fighter's lead punch against a left-handed opponent is a right, then he puts himself in a dangerous position when his lead misses: His right hand and arm are fully extended, so he cannot protect himself from an oncoming punch when his opponent strikes back with a left. It is basic boxing strategy to lead with the left against a left-handed boxer, and Ali followed this strategy to perfection.

By the third round, Frazier had thrown an awful lot of punches at Ali's body, most of which Ali had deflected or had been absorbed by his arms, elbows, or gloves. Ali then chose to stop bouncing off the ropes; he stood flat-footed and traded swings with Frazier. When he backed Frazier across the ring, he spoke to the fighter. He told Frazier that he had not been hurt by him and then taunted Frazier to come at him.

Their vicious toe-to-toe fighting continued in the fourth round, when Frazier hit Ali with a clean shot to the head that drew first blood. Frazier soon began to dominate. He hit Ali's body and then caught him with a couple of straight jabs to the head.

By the fifth round, it was Frazier's turn to taunt Ali. He held his hands low and let Ali take shots at him, many of which missed. At the end of the round, he derided Ali by patting him on the top of his head.

The rhythm of the fight flattened out in the sixth, seventh, and eighth rounds. Frazier continued to work on Ali's body with thunderous hooks to the ribs, and the two fighters traded occasional jabs to the head.

In the ninth round, the tempo of the fight changed dramatically when Ali stunned Frazier with a hook. Ali was suddenly all over Frazier, who wobbled around the ring and covered up his face with his gloves. The triumph of Ali's rope-a-dope tactics appeared imminent. However, he could not put Frazier away.

When the bell rang, Frazier stumbled to his corner. He was given smelling salts to clear his head, and water was toweled over his body to refresh him. Ali would later regret not finishing off Frazier in the ninth round.

In the 10th round, Ali was too tired from his exertion in the previous round, and Frazier was too cautious and stunned to repeat another direct confrontation. While both fighters threw an occasional leaden punch, this and the next round provided time for them to gather their strength.

Frazier, who was visibly worn out but showed tremendous heart, came back strong in the 12th round. He launched an all-out attack on Ali, hitting him with right-jab–left-hook combinations that shook him but did not knock him out. These blows marked the last burst of energy from either fighter. During the next two rounds, they seemed to waltz around the ring, hanging on to each other like drunken dinosaurs.

Just when it appeared as though the fight would end without a climax, a wild left hook—Frazier's best punch—near the end of the 15th and final round sent Ali thudding to the canvas. Frazier stared in disbelief as Ali tried to pick himself off the mat. The referee moved in to give Ali a count. The crowd began to roar.

Ali made it to his feet, and for a moment both fighters just stared at each other. Seconds later, the fight was over. Ali and Frazier went to their respective corners and collapsed on their stools, waiting as the judges huddled together to total their scores for the fight. A microphone was eventually placed before the ring announcer, who said in time-honored fashion, "Ladies and gentlemen . . ." and proceeded to read out the points given by the judges before announcing their decision,". . . and still the champion, Joe Frazier."

It had been, according to the *Times*, a "monumental epic fight." Yet it was also Ali's first loss in a professional fight. Frazier was still the champion.

The fight was a stunning reversal for Ali. Suddenly, he seemed human again. He was not invincible; he could be beaten by a tough and determined fighter. Nevertheless, it had taken a superhuman effort by Frazier for him to win. Ali was still a major contender—perhaps *the* major contender—for the championship. Knowing this, Frazier and his advisers would avoid scheduling a rematch with Ali for as long as they could.

Three and a half months after Ali lost the title bout, he won his political freedom. On June 28, 1971, the Supreme Court ruled unanimously that his conviction was invalid. He was subsequently granted the status of conscientious objector to the military draft on the grounds of his religious beliefs.

The Supreme Court vindicated Ali by ruling against the government on three points. First, the court found that Ali's objection to serving in the armed forces was based on religious training and belief. (The government had claimed that Ali's desire to avoid the draft was not based on religious grounds.) Second, the court rejected the government's claim that Ali was not sincere in his beliefs. Third, the court dismissed as irrelevant the government's claim that Ali was not opposed to all wars. The court found that the last point had not been an issue in the government's case during the first appeal in New Orleans and thus, by procedure and tradition, should not be considered by the Supreme Court, either.

With the issue of his draft status resolved once and for all, Ali could devote his full attention to regaining the heavyweight title. In a sense, he was in the same position after the Frazier fight as he had been before he was able to fight for the title against Liston in 1964: He had to prove himself by methodically fighting his way to another championship match. However, there was one main difference between his path to the title in 1964 and the one he had to take in 1971. In 1964, Liston had taken Ali too lightly and had paid the price. The second time around, the handful of top contenders knew how good Ali was and tried to avoid him.

Ali took part in three more fights in 1971 and in six fights in 1972. He won all of them, including six by knockout. On January 22, 1973, Frazier was dethroned by former Olympic gold medalist George Foreman. To Frazier, the loss of the title meant that he might be more willing to fight Ali.

Ali proceeded with his climb back to the top of the boxing world by fighting a little-known boxer named Ken Norton in San Diego, California, in March 1973. Ali did not take Norton as seriously as he should have. He also had some especially bad luck on the night of the fight, which took place in Norton's home state.

Norton swung wildly and not very expertly throughout the entire fight. In the first round, he landed what Ali felt was a lucky punch to the side of his face. The punch broke Ali's jaw. Not wanting to give his opponent a psychological lift, Ali did not show any reaction, even though he was in terrible pain.

Ali signs for a second match with Ken Norton (left) after losing a 12-round fight to him on March 31, 1973. By winning the rematch on September 10, 1973, Ali took a major step toward winning the heavyweight title for a second time.

However, the pain caused Ali to lose his concentration, and he was not very sharp. Norton beat him to the punch during most of the fight. Ali never mounted an effective counterattack to Norton's aggressive style, although he managed to last through all 12 rounds of the fight. The judges ruled in favor of Norton, the local favorite. The fight, which was Ali's second professional loss, caused many commentators to agree with sportswriter William Wallace's

assessment in the *Times* that "it was all very sad—
the beginning of the end of the line" for Ali.

However, Ali would not allow himself to be put
into retirement so easily. He immediately booked a
rematch with Norton for the following September in
Los Angeles. Yet he continued to be jinxed by Norton. In the sixth round, he broke a bone in his hand
while hitting Norton, and he had to fight mostly one-
handed for the remainder of the bout. Still, Ali beat

Norton by putting on a smart, classic boxing exhibition that confused his opponent and clearly demonstrated Ali's superiority as a fighter.

By beating Norton, Ali set himself up for his second major fight since the end of his exile. He signed with Frazier for a rematch, to be held again at Madison Square Garden, on January 28, 1974. It was understood that the winner of this match would then meet Foreman for the heavyweight championship.

Ali was eager for a second fight with Frazier. "I think we should do it again," he said, "because we draw more people to an event than anybody in the recorded history of records." His estimation was not far off. While he would not clear the $2.5 million he made from his first fight with Frazier, he did receive $1.7 million for the fight, which was billed as Ali-Frazier II. It was his largest payday in almost three years.

The first Ali-Frazier fight had gone 15 rounds; their rematch was scheduled for a merciful 12 rounds. Ali had learned a few things about Frazier during their first fight—the most important point being that he would get nowhere playing rope-a-dope with the roughhousing Philadelphian. Instead, he chose to box Frazier.

During their rematch, Ali was seldom on the ropes. Instead, he danced a little and clinched a lot. Whenever the referee pried him away from Frazier, Ali jabbed him as he moved.

Ali almost won the fight near the end of the second round with a solid left hook that knocked Frazier to the floor. Unfortunately for Ali, someone yelled out, "Bell." This cry confused the referee, who stopped the fight for almost 20 seconds. The pause gave Frazier enough time to get off the canvas and clear his head. However, this brief respite proved to be of little help to Frazier. Ali eluded him for most

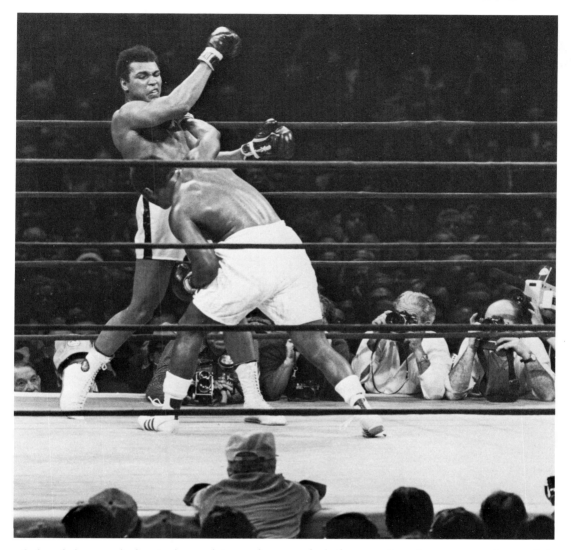

of the fight, and the judges ultimately awarded the victory to Ali.

Sportswriter Red Smith reported that the two fighters "came in as former champions, both beaten, both past their prime." However, Smith was right only on one point—that they both had been beaten before. Ali was about to show the world that he was far from being a has-been. **《⌾》**

The judges unanimously awarded the victory to Ali at the end of his second confrontation with Joe Frazier (shown here), held on January 28, 1974.

8

THE GREATEST

ALI'S INCESSANT DESIRE to push himself further than he has ever been took him in 1974 to a large, modern structure built in a clearing in the jungle outside Kinshasa, Zaire, in Africa. The structure, known as 20th of May Stadium, had the look of an American football arena. Yet there was also something sinister about it.

For one thing, the stadium was already beginning to decay even though it was only a few years old. The ruin was subtle yet pervasive: Bits of concrete had fallen off the structure; weeds were growing at various places in the floor; cracks had appeared in some of the support columns. The stadium had been built quickly, shoddily, and expensively as a symbol of the potency of one of Africa's most long-lived and brutal dictatorships, the reign of Colonel Joseph Mobutu.

It was both proper and ironic that Ali's destiny led him to Zaire, on the continent of his ancestors. It was proper because he had always taken great pride in his African ancestry and encouraged other black Americans to do likewise. It was ironic because the reason for his visit to Zaire, which was to fight Foreman, proved to be one of the greatest promotional hypes in boxing history.

The Rumble in the Jungle, as the Ali-Foreman fight was dubbed, was the result of Mobutu's attempt to gain respectability for his country and an American

Ali's claim that he is "the Greatest" was borne out when he was awarded a diamond-studded belt for being the top professional athlete of 1974.

President Joseph Mobutu (center) introduces George Foreman (left) and Ali to the people of Zaire before their "Rumble in the Jungle" on October 30, 1974.

boxing promoter's urge for a flamboyant and money-making promotion. Mobutu of Zaire and promoter Don King of Cleveland had little knowledge of one another before Ali's rematch with Frazier at Madison Square Garden. However, following Ali's victory, the greed and vanity that led eventually to the slugfest at 20th of May Stadium were soon set in motion.

King was the one promoter who had the connections to put together an Ali-Foreman fight. Ali was ready to take on Foreman, but the champion and his managers were reluctant to meet Ali. When King found out through Muhammad that the nation of Zaire had offered money guarantees for as much as $5 million for each fighter, he knew he would be able to get Foreman to sign a contract for the fight.

Agents of the two fighters met with Zairian representatives until they finally reached an agreement.

All sorts of organizations and individuals had staged and promoted fights in the 100 years since the advent of modern boxing, but Zaire became the first national government to accept these roles. The fight was to be held in early October 1974, and the two fighters were each guaranteed $5 million.

Ali faced an awesome, though not thoroughly tested, opponent in Foreman. He was big; at 220–225 pounds, he was bigger than Ali, bigger than Frazier, and even more of a bear than Liston, who had been one of Foreman's heroes. Like Liston, he enjoyed knocking out his opponents early. He had needed only a total of 11½ minutes—less than four complete rounds—to dispatch Joe "King" Roman, Frazier, and Norton. Also like Liston, Foreman was a hard puncher. His favorite punch was his "anywhere" punch, so named because "anywhere it hits you it breaks something inside you." This punch could be either a right or left hook—usually to the body. Either hook was devastating. The writer Norman Mailer, who covered the fight in Zaire, described Foreman's main weapon as a "a big hook, heavy as death, oppressive as the closing of one's tomb."

Ali was not frightened by the prospect of going against such a hard-hitting young fighter. If anything, he relished the challenge. Even though critics had said that Ali was finished and that at 32 he was too old to fight, he knew he was not like other boxers. He had extraordinary intuitive skills that told him when to lay back and when to push ahead.

In addition, if Ali beat Foreman, he would become only the second man ever to win the heavyweight title twice. The other fighter to do this was Floyd Patterson. No one had ever won it three times.

Because others said that Ali was too old to fight and because winning meant being the heavyweight champion once again, he drove himself relentlessly to prepare himself for the bout. He trained the entire summer before the match at his camp in the mountains of Pennsylvania, and he arrived in Zaire a month before the fight to acclimatize himself to the smothering African heat. He was looking forward to regaining the title that had been taken away from him in 1967, when he was at the peak of his career.

Foreman suffered a cut over his eye during a sparring session, and the fight had to be postponed for a few weeks. By the night of the fight, October 30, Ali was—both physically and psychologically—in the best shape since the end of his exile. The match was broadcast via satellite to closed-circuit television venues in America as well as to theaters and halls in many other countries of the world. To accommodate the American audience, the fight began in Zaire at a weird hour: 2:00 A.M.

As many as 80,000 spectators jammed into 20th of May Stadium. In the United States, the bout was viewed by millions more in sold-out theaters across the country. Former boxing champions Jack Dempsey

Ali trained especially hard for his bout with George Foreman, knowing that a victory would give him the heavyweight championship for a second time.

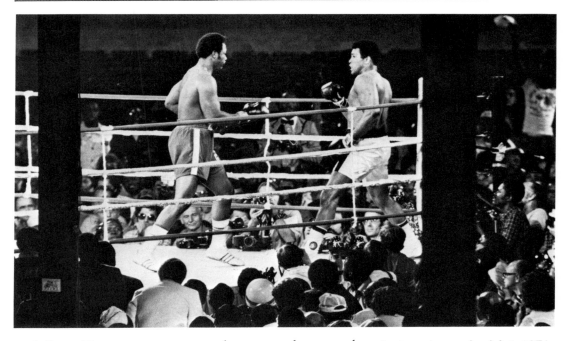

and Gene Tunney were among the many who turned out to watch a less than perfect broadcast on a giant screen in Madison Square Garden, where the shifting images that appeared on the screen in front of them seemed as though they could have been filmed on the moon rather than in equatorial Africa.

To the cheers of *"Ali bomaye!"* (which roughly means "Kill him, Ali!"), the older fighter made his way down the aisle to the ring. He was dressed in natty white satin boxing trunks with black piping and a white silk African robe. Foreman entered next, wearing his characteristic patriotic colors: red velvet trunks with white stripes and a blue waistband. As the referee read the rules, Ali started to work on the psyche of Foreman, telling him, "You have heard of me since you were young. You've been following me since you were a little boy. Now you meet me, your master."

At the sound of the opening bell, the two fighters charged out of their corners, ran up to each other, and backed away as if repelled by magnetic force.

In the early rounds of their 1974 heavyweight championship fight in Zaire, George Foreman (left) backed Ali into a corner and began to deliver his trademark "anywhere punches."

The action in the 1974 "Rumble in the Jungle" turned in Ali's favor in the middle rounds, as he began to overwhelm a tiring George Foreman (left).

They stalked each other around the ring, feeling each other out; then Ali got in the first two blows—hard rights to Foreman's head—before tying him up in a clinch to ward off a counterpunch. Foreman disengaged from Ali and, as he had been trained to do, followed Ali around the ring, lumbering after him like a rhinoceros, cutting him off at the corners so that he could not dance away. Once he had cut off Ali, he attacked with right and left haymakers to the body—anywhere punches. Ali felt them.

Ali realized quickly that Foreman was well trained in stopping his movement. He responded instinctively by moving to the ropes, where he covered himself as well as he could while Foreman unloaded his doomsday punches. Ali was playing rope-a-dope again—only this time, unlike the first Frazier fight, he was in perfect condition.

For some reason, the ropes had not been wound as tightly as they should have been. This gave Ali room in which to work. He often leaned far back into the ropes so that he could dodge or better absorb Foreman's blows. Nevertheless, he knew that playing rope-a-dope would put him in trouble if the fight went the full 15 rounds.

Ali followed his instinct to play rope-a-dope during the first three rounds even though Dundee was screaming at him from his corner to move, to dance. He also kept up the chatter directed at Foreman, telling him, among other things, "Shoot your best shot."

Foreman's best shots were almost enough to finish the fight. Several of them took Ali to the threshold of a place he has described as the "dream room." According to Ali, when a fighter receives a jolting blow, the door to the dream room "opens, and you see neon orange and green lights blinking. You see bats blowing trumpets; alligators play trombones; and snakes are screaming. Weird masks and actor's clothes hang on the wall." Because Ali had seen these things before, he did not panic. He shot a few right jabs—leads—off Foreman's head; he surprised Foreman with these right leads because they exposed his body and thus go against the norm of boxing.

In the fourth and fifth rounds, Foreman began to tire in the sultry African heat, and Ali rose to the attack. He popped off the ropes more often, hitting Foreman with smart combinations that snapped his head around. As Ali began to move, Foreman followed, but he was no longer the determined rhinoceros of the early rounds. Instead, he plodded after Ali. He had clearly grown leg weary.

By the seventh round, Ali began to dominate the fight, striking Foreman with a number of quick jabs. However, his body hurt from Foreman's earlier punches, and he knew that Foreman's second wind might come soon. So Ali stayed off the ropes and began to press the attack in the eighth round.

Ali receives some advice from his trainer, Angelo Dundee, between rounds of his 1974 heavyweight championship match against George Foreman in Zaire.

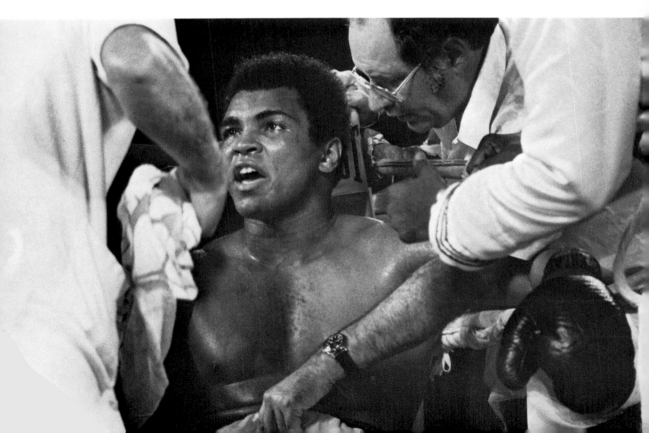

Just before the bell, Ali hit Foreman with a right-left-right combination that staggered the younger fighter. He tiptoed to the ropes, doubtlessly seeing the laughing lizards and bats playing saxophone for the first time in his career. Pinned against the ropes, as Ali had been in the first rounds, Foreman was hit with the coup de grace: three big rights that sent him on a slow-motion odyssey around the ring one last time, until he collapsed slowly; it took a full 20 seconds for him to fall into a heap in the center of the canvas.

Not one single person in the stadium remained in his seat. On the large screen in Madison Square Garden, the voices of the announcers were drowned out by the cheers. In the flickering light of the arena, the New York crowd heard only two words being chanted over and over again: *"Ali bomaye!"*

In his dressing room after the fight, a jubilant Ali said, "I told you he was nothing, but did you listen. . . . I told you I was the greatest of all time. Never again say I'm the underdog until I'm 50 years of age."

This last statement by Ali was classic playacting. He had quietly announced before the bout that he was considering retirement after the Foreman fight, win or lose. It was the first time that he had ever mentioned retirement.

In the flush of victory after the match, Ali decided to keep on fighting. He would ring in a few more bouts and enjoy some large paydays. After all, he was the champion once again; he might as well enjoy the privileges that came with being at the top.

Ali figured that he could quit whenever he wanted to. Yet he would find that it would be harder to do so than to become champion. The lure of the limelight and the big sums of money he was making would keep him fighting for longer than was good for him. But for the time being, who could argue with his

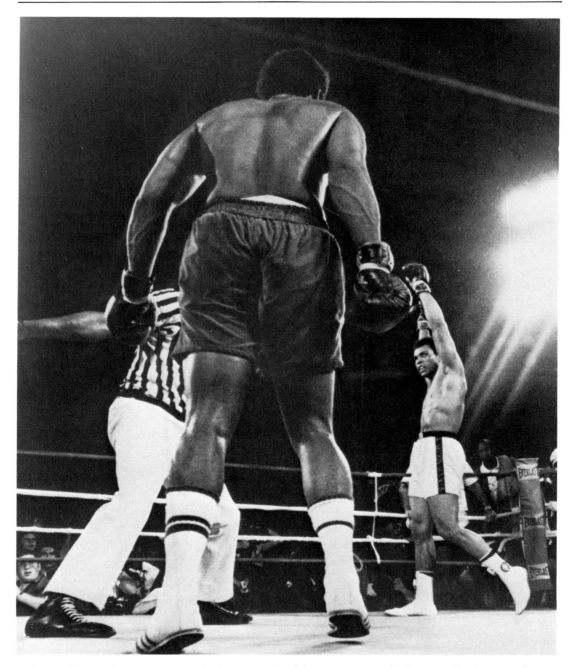

A beaten George Foreman (center) looks on as Ali celebrates regaining the heavyweight championship title.

While Ali was training in the Philippines for his third bout with Joe Frazier, he was accompanied by Veronica Porche (left), who later became his third wife.

decision to continue fighting? He had triumphed over his opponents, over the U.S. government, over age, seemingly over mortality itself. He was, as he himself said, the Greatest.

The Foreman fight was Ali's last bout in 1974. The following year, he fought four times. Three of these fights were against much lesser opponents; the last fight was against Frazier. Ali never made less than $1 million for each of these bouts. For the Frazier fight, held in the Philippines, he earned $4 million.

Ali began to train less often after the Foreman fight. Training was the toughest part of boxing as well as the least glamorous. However, the routine was indispensable for preparing a fighter's body and mind for the sport.

Ali did not even bother to spar for the Frazier fight. Instead, he began to indulge himself in the high life with the money he was making. He ate well and put on weight. Although he usually took most of it off before a match, he never regained the conditioning he had achieved for the Foreman fight.

Ali also began to see women other than his second wife, Belinda. By the time he established a training camp in Manila in the Philippines for the Frazier fight, he and Belinda were close to a divorce. Ali introduced his companion of the moment, Veronica Porche, as his wife to the president of the Philippines, Ferdinand Marcos. This gaffe was picked up by the U.S. newspapers the week before the fight. Ali reacted angrily to the news coverage of his private life, saying, "This is going too far. They got me for the draft. They got me for my religion. They got me for all sorts of things. But they shouldn't be able to get me for my girlfriend."

The third Ali-Frazier bout, known as the Thrilla in Manila, was held on October 1, 1975. Ali's last truly great fight, the match was a wild, seesaw affair, with first one man taking control, then the other. In this respect, it was much like the other two fights between them.

Perhaps because Ali was not in the best of shape, it was he—and not Frazier—who came out quickly, looking for the early knockout. Ali dominated the first rounds, but Frazier, as always, was doggedly determined to win and turned the contest into a ferocious fight. By the 14th round, Frazier's face resembled a lumpy peach. His eyes were almost swollen shut, and he could scarcely walk. His trainer, Eddie Futch, stopped the fight by not letting his man come out for the bell in the 15th round.

When it was all over, Ali knew that he had fought his toughest fight. Although he had won, he may have damaged himself in the process. After the fight, he commented, "You may have seen the last of Ali. I want to get out. I'm tired and on top. What you saw tonight was next to death. He's [Frazier] the toughest man in the world."

After Ali's courageous performance, Red Smith, who had not always been a fan of Ali's, wrote in the *Times*:

> Say what you will about this noisy extrovert, this swaggering, preening, play-acting slice of theatrical ham: the man is a gladiator. He was a callow braggart of 22 when Sonny Liston surrendered the title to him 11 years ago. At the ripe age of 33 he is a champion of genuine quality.

Ali did not fight again for almost a whole year. When he finally came back to the ring, he made it worth his while. The fight was against Norton—their third match. It was held at Yankee Stadium in New York on a cool night on September 28, 1976. Ali was guaranteed a record $6 million for the bout. The live gate brought in $3.5 million, breaking the long-standing record of $2.6 million established by the Jack Dempsey–Gene Tunney fight held at Soldier Field in Chicago almost a half century earlier.

On October 1, 1975, Ali battled Joe Frazier (left) for 14 rounds before defeating him for the second time in three meetings. Ali considered the "Thrilla in Manila" to be his toughest championship fight.

Ali was cocky as usual before the fight. Even though he was in awful shape, he predicted a knockout in five rounds. The fight went the full 15 rounds again, and throughout the fight, Ali never threw a punch that hurt Norton. He outboxed Ali in most of the rounds.

However, at the end of the match, the judges awarded the victory to Ali—reigning champions are rarely voted against in a fight that goes the distance. James J. Braddock had been the last reigning heavyweight champion deposed by the judges' verdict. That

At the age of 34, Ali put an end to the talk of his retiring from boxing by agreeing to fight Ken Norton for the third time.

had taken place 41 years before, in a fight against Max Schmeling. Before Braddock, only two other heavyweight champions had lost a verdict: Schmeling to Dempsey in 1932 and Dempsey to Tunney in 1926.

Ali accepted the decision and the money, but uncharacteristically, he had little to say after the fight. However, several days later, on a visit to Turkey with Wallace Muhammad, the eldest son of Elijah Muhammad, who had become the new leader of the Nation of Islam after his father's death, Ali announced his retirement from boxing. He was going to dedicate himself to the Islamic cause. Whether or not he stayed out of the ring for good would depend on how much money he was offered to fight again and, perhaps even more importantly, the requirements of his ego. ⚬

Ali announced his initial retirement from the ring and his intention to dedicate himself completely to Islam while he was visiting religious shrines in Turkey in 1976.

9
THE
CHAMPION
OF CHANGE

ALI MADE A sincere effort to devote his life exclusively to Islam. Spurred on by Wallace Muhammad's challenge that he "use his power—the fist of his tongue, instead of the fist of the ring—for truth," he traveled all over to talk about his experiences since his conversion to Islam. However, the thrill of adulation, once experienced, was hard to leave behind. In addition, the money was still there, waiting to be picked up at the stroke of a pen; all Ali had to do was sign a contract to fight. He was away from the ring for only seven months.

Ali's first fight after his retirement took place on May 16, 1977, in Landover, Maryland, against Alfredo Evangelista. When another heavyweight champion, Joe Louis, had run out of worthy opponents in the late 1930s, he began to fight what the press labeled "a bum a month." Evangelista was the sort of fighter who, had he practiced his trade in Louis's day, probably would have been put into that same category.

Although Ali had retired from the ring, he had never taken the final steps that were required of him to renounce his championship; also, less than a year had passed since his last title defense. Because of these two facts, he was still considered to be the undisputed

Few people are as well known around the world as Ali. He is shown here playfully trading punches with a Chinese youth in Peking.

heavyweight champion—and as the champion, he was able to command a lordly $2.5 million guarantee for the Evangelista match. Ali's choice of Evangelista, who was not a top contender, as his next opponent indicated that the current heavyweight champion might have learned from Louis how to pick up some easy money.

Ali began training for Evangelista about eight weeks before the fight. When the champion set up training camp, he weighed in at a bloated 240 pounds. He managed to slim down to a respectable 221 pounds by the day of the official fight weigh-in.

Ali in his prime would have taken four or five rounds to destroy Evangelista, but at the age of 35, he was not able to finish off his opponent. The fight went the full 15 rounds. Ali was not sharp; he moved ponderously around the ring. He clinched and covered up well, and he managed to keep Evangelista at a distance during most of the fight. But his punches had little power.

In spite of Ali's pitiful performance, he won the fight on the judges' decision—the tradition that a reigning heavyweight champion does not lose a fight on points held up. Sportswriter Randy Newmann noted in the *Times*:

> Ali, being a living legend, is a hometown fighter wherever he fights. The world is his backyard. Only he can score points lying on the ropes, dancing around. . . . Beating Ali by decision is like giving Jack Nicklaus a stroke a ball. You're beat before you start.

However, an unusual and disturbing pattern in Ali's fights was becoming evident. As he grew older, he was having to fight longer. He had not been able to win any of his last six fights—including the Evangelista bout—before the 11th round. Ali's doctor, Ferdie Pacheco, noted after the champion faced Evangelista, "Ali is now at the dangerous mental point where his heart and mind are no longer in it. . . . It's just a payday. It's almost as if an actor played his role too long. He's just mouthing the words."

Ignoring his poor showing and the danger to his health that had been alluded to by Pacheco, Ali continued his routine of picking up a few million dollars every eight months or so. He also found some new ways to keep himself in the public eye. In 1977, he starred in *The Greatest*, the film version of his autobiography. The following year, he lent his name and voice to "Muhammad Ali," a television cartoon series for children.

On February 15, 1978, Ali fought another so-called bum of the month, the largely unknown Leon Spinks. More than 10 years younger than the 36-year-old Ali, he was a former marine from St. Louis, Missouri, with only seven professional fights to his credit. Although he possessed a wild, awkward boxing

Ali was confident when he entered his championship match against Leon Spinks (right) on February 15, 1978, that the fight would result in an easy victory. However, Spinks surprised Ali and most of the boxing world by winning on a judges' decision.

style, he was hungry for the crown. "I'm a pecking chicken," he told reporters, "and Ali's got the gold I really want."

However, to many sportswriters, Spinks, who had fought such nonentities as "Lightning" Bob Smith and Scott LeDoux, seemed destined for oblivion rather than for the heavyweight crown. To these writers, his toughest fight seemed to have been the one he once had with his brother Michael, who was also a fighter, over a baloney sandwich. Accordingly, an Ali-Spinks fight seemed like more than a little baloney, too.

Ali's fight against Spinks also went the full 15 rounds. However, Spinks—unlike Evangelista or Norton—was all over Ali throughout the fight, trapping him in the corners and pounding him, breaking through his peak-a-boo crouch. Ali tried to dance,

After Leon Spinks took the heavyweight title from Ali, the 36-year-old boxer quickly set up a rematch. He is shown here vowing to win the heavyweight crown for an unprecedented third time.

but his feet would not respond. Instead, he dragged himself around the ring.

At the end of the fight, boxing tradition was shattered. For the first time in 43 years, a reigning champion lost a judges' decision. Spinks became the new heavyweight champion of the world.

The loss to Spinks seemed to awaken Ali. He demanded and received a rematch with the young champion, which was set for September 15, 1978, in New Orleans. To get back in shape, Ali set a grueling training regimen for himself. He rented a secluded bungalow on Lake Ponchatrain in Louisiana in late July and ran three to five miles every day. He worked on strengthening his torso by doing 12 different kinds of sit-ups; one of his assistant trainers estimated he did 8,000 sit-ups in the month and a half that preceded the fight. He also set up a special diet for himself: He began every day with two trout, eggs, and unbuttered toast; he then washed down salt, iron, and potassium tablets with a glass of orange juice. He also had an emotional and psychological advantage to help him along with his training: If he beat Spinks, he would become the first heavyweight ever to win the title three times. .

While Ali was rebuilding, Spinks was busy at work destroying himself. Spink's hangers-on had persuaded him to fire George Benton, the manager who had helped him become the champion. Sam Solomon, one of Spinks's buddies, replaced Benton. However, Solomon did not have a plan for Spinks to follow when fighting Ali. Solomon was also very lax when it came to handling the fantastically undisciplined young boxer.

Two weeks before the fight was to take place, Spinks's brother Michael called Benton back in to help; it had become obvious that the young champion was unprepared for the fight. But the call for help was already too late; Solomon would not give up his job. Consequently, Benton and Solomon worked out a ludicrous deal that split the management of Spinks's fight between them: They would trade the duty of managing Spinks during every other round of the fight.

"I've said this many times before about Ali," Benton warned about the fighter's combination of luck, skill, and determination. "Liston. Foreman. Frazier. The draft thing. Ali always comes up on his feet. It's like there's some mystical force guiding his life, making him not like other men. When I think of that . . . it's scary."

Seven days before the fight, Spinks disappeared into the seedy bars of New Orleans. He was finally found several days later and was brought back to his camp to sober up. However, the night before the fight, he stayed up until the wee hours of the morning, drinking with his friends and some women who had attached themselves to his camp.

The final act of unprofessionalism in the Spinks camp occurred just before the bout. While dressing for the fight in the locker room, Spinks discovered that his entourage had forgotten to bring his protective cup, water bucket, and water bottles. He had to borrow this equipment from another fighter.

Ali came out in the first round determined to give Spinks a boxing lesson. The veteran fought an elegant fight—not overpowering (he was too old to manage that) but stylish. He circled left and jabbed repeatedly, hitting Spinks's head as though it were a speed bag. When Ali, who outweighed Spinks by 20 pounds, became the target of a Spinks charge, he rudely grabbed the younger man, held him in a clinch for a while, then pushed him away so that he could jab him some more.

By the fifth round, Ali was stinging Spinks with a combination of punches, and Spinks was openly looking to his corner for advice. But Benton, who had become fed up with the alternating-round system of managing, had left the auditorium during that round, not to return. Although the fight went the full 15 rounds, no one was surprised when the ringside announcer intoned after it was over that the new heavyweight champion of the world was Ali. An impressed Spinks said after the fight, "He was always my idol. He still is."

Having won the heavyweight championship for a third time, Ali was now ready to retire. The physical ordeal of boxing was becoming too much for him, and now that he was older, the glitter of stardom finally seemed less important to him than it had once been. He said:

> God, I have suffered and suffered and suffered. It really hurts. It's time for a new life. . . . I don't want to fight no more. I've been doing it for 25 years and you can only do so much wear to the body. It changes a man. It has changed me. I can see it. I can feel it.

Ali defeated Leon Spinks (right) with an impressive demonstration of boxing skills on September 15, 1978, thus capturing the world heavyweight title for the third time.

Ali with his and wife Veronica's first daughter.

Ali remained in retirement for two full years. During that time, he settled down in his homes in Chicago and Los Angeles and seemed to be content conducting business deals and living with Veronica Porche, who had become his third wife, and their two children. His career earnings totaled an estimated $50 million. However, in 1980, his need for money and attention compelled him into the ring once again. His opponent was Larry Holmes, one of the sparring partners whom he had brought to Africa when he had taken the title from Foreman.

Ali was 38 years old and overweight at the time of the Holmes fight, which proved to be an embarrassment for him. The match was held in the 100-degree heat of Las Vegas and lasted 11 rounds before Herbert Muhammad stopped it. Ali threw only a couple of punches during the whole fight; these punches seemed to be so weak that they would not have hurt a child. Holmes, who respected Ali, treated the champion as gently as he could. But by the end of the fight, Ali had suffered a bloody nose, a cut under his right eye, and reddening under his left eye.

Ali claimed that his sluggish performance had resulted from a drug, Thyrolar, which he had been taking for a thyroid condition. He had lately been displaying alarming physical abnormalities. His speech had become noticeably slurred, and he seemed to drag his feet slightly when he walked. However, the former champion laughed off questions about his general physical condition and stated that he was feeling fine.

Ali certainly appeared to be doing well financially. He owned valuable real estate; he dressed well and traveled often. The one blot in his business affairs was his association with an organization that carried his name but with which he was not involved in any other way. In 1981, Harold Smith, the president and chairman of Muhammad Ali Professional Sports, Inc., found himself at the center of a scandal that involved the embezzlement of $21.3 million from a Los Angeles branch of the Wells Fargo Bank. Smith, who went into hiding for a number of months after being sought for questioning, claimed that he was innocent of embezzlement charges and stated that he had bought the use of Ali's name for $1 million. Ali, who said that Smith had only paid him $200,000, broke his ties with the organization after the scandal erupted.

In 1981, Ali made his last attempt at a boxing comeback—only to discover that none of the major boxers wanted to fight him. Even if they had, none of the boxing commissions in any state would have given him a license to box due to his less than perfect health. Yet Ali eventually managed to get a permit to box in the Bahamas. On December 11, 1981, he fought and lost a 10-round match against Trevor Berbick. Ali, who weighed in for the fight at 237 pounds,

Fight promoter Don King (center) separates Ali and challenger Larry Holmes (left) as the two fighters publicize their heavyweight title bout set for October 2, 1980.

Ali and fellow Muslims at prayer. His devotion to the Muslim faith has helped to guide him through his often controversial career.

performed better than he had against Holmes. He even managed to stagger Berbick in the fifth round. However, Berbick won easily on the judges' decision.

Ali certainly should not have fought against Holmes and Berbick. Perhaps he did so to prove to himself that he was still vital and young. Actually, he was neither—as would be attested to three years later. In September 1984, he was hospitalized for diagnostic tests to determine the cause of his worsening speech slur, listlessness, and difficulty in movement. Doctors at Columbia-Presbyterian Hospital in New York City discovered that Ali was suffering from Parkinson's syndrome, which manifests symptoms of Parkinson's disease. Ali's illness had been brought about by blows that had been delivered to his head during his boxing career.

If left untreated, Parkinson's disease usually becomes a degenerative disease; its effects will become worse over time, until its victim is severely handicapped. However, even though Parkinson's disease cannot be cured, its symptoms—stooped posture, slurred speech, tremor of the hands, a short-stepped gait, and slowness of movement—can be successfully treated with a group of drugs called L-dopa. This is the medication that was prescribed for Ali by the doctors at Columbia-Presbyterian Hospital.

Ali's hospitalization and the death of several fighters resulting from blows they suffered in the ring touched off a furor among physicians and the general public about boxing's role in society. Two prestigious medical publications, the *Journal of the American Medical Association* and the British journal *Lancet*, have recently released studies documenting the dangers of a career in boxing. The American Medical Association article reported on a study of 38 former boxers: More than half had suffered damage or loss of brain tissue. Tissue loss is especially dangerous because it can lead to the state of physical and mental impairment known as punch-drunk syndrome (called *dementia pugilistica* by doctors). The symptoms of punch-drunk syndrome are memory loss, eye and ear problems, slurred speech, an abnormal gait, and tremors. *Lancet* summed up its findings by stating that "the most predictable and permanent reward of a career in boxing is chronic

An American ambassador of international goodwill, Ali has traveled to the four corners of the earth. He is shown here meeting with Soviet premier Leonid Brezhnev (right) in Moscow.

brain damage." These two studies have added more fuel to a movement to ban boxing.

Even though Ali is now suffering from the effects of his boxing career, he does not believe boxing should be banned. He reasons that in a society in which blacks and other minorities are given too few opportunities for advancement, boxing offers a way out of poverty. He has said, "Too many blacks are doing well in boxing, so whites want it banned. But how do I live here [gesturing to his house and antiques] without boxing. There's more deaths in football than boxing, but nobody wants to ban football. You see car races. Cars hit the wall, burn up. . . . Don't ban that, do they?"

Although Ali still defends boxing, his days as a boxer are over. There will be no more ill-advised comeback attempts. "My avocation is business," he now says. As of 1987, he was involved in real-estate development, a shoe-polish company, and the perfume business. His grandest business venture, though, has been in automobiles. He has a joint partnership with Brazilian investors, Volkswagen of Brazil, and Sheik Mohammad Al Fassi to manufacture and sell cars to the Arab and American markets. One model to be sold in Egypt and Saudi Arabia is called the Al Fassi; another, a fast sports car destined for America, is fittingly named the Ali Stinger.

Ventures such as these have helped Ali to continue on his path of success. He still has the same pride and admirable stubbornness that drove him to become a wealthy man and arguably the finest boxer ever to step into the ring. But even more important than the wealth and personal glory he has attained, Ali has left a lasting legacy to America: the strong, positive image of black America that he has always insisted on presenting to the world. Sportswriter Steve Cady explained the importance of this legacy in the *Times* by saying:

Like so many other black people I love Ali because he is intolerable to America. His significance to me is a thousandfold. For a black man to exist he must be the greatest. He must say it over and over again, because white people might forget.

After being treated for Parkinson's syndrome, Ali meets with reporters to announce that he is still "the Greatest."

Muhammad Ali will not let anyone forget who he is and where he came from. Perhaps this—more than any knockout in the ring—has been his greatest achievement. ◀◆▶

CHRONOLOGY

——— ✿ ———

Jan. 18, 1942	Born Cassius Clay, Jr., in Louisville Kentucky
1954	Takes his first boxing lesson
1955	Appears in the Kentucky State Golden Gloves tournament
1959	Wins national Golden Gloves tournament
1960	Wins Golden Gloves, Amateur Athletic Union championship, and Olympic gold medal as a light heavyweight; signs with the Louisville Millionaires
1964	Beats Sonny Liston in six rounds for the heavyweight championship; announces his conversion to Islam and changes his name to Muhammad Ali
1967	Refuses induction into the armed forces; is convicted for draft evasion; boxing license is revoked and is stripped of heavyweight title
1970	Beats Jerry Quarry in three rounds
1971	Loses to Joe Frazier in 15 rounds for first professional loss
1974	Beats Frazier in 12 rounds; beats George Foreman in eight rounds and gains heavyweight title
1975	Beats Frazier in 14 rounds
1978	Loses heavyweight title to Spinks in 15 rounds; beats Spinks in 15 rounds to regain heavyweight title for third time
1980	Loses to Larry Holmes in 11 rounds
1981	Loses to Trevor Berbick in 10 rounds; retires from boxing
1984	Is diagnosed as suffering from Parkinson's syndrome

FURTHER READING

Ali, Muhammad. *The Greatest: My Own Story.* New York: Random House, 1975.

Mailer, Norman. *The Fight.* Boston: Little, Brown, 1975.

Schulberg, Bud. *Loser and Still Champion: Muhammad Ali.* New York: Doubleday, 1972.

Sheed, Wilfrid. *Muhammad Ali.* New York: Crowell, 1975.

Torres, Jose. *Sting Like a Bee: The Muhammad Ali Story.* New York: Abelard-Schuman, 1975.

INDEX

Ali, Muhammad (Cassius Clay)
  amateur career, 23, 27, 29,
    30
  banned from boxing, 62–63,
    65–66, 68–69, 71–74
  birth, 15
  Black Muslims and, 44, 45,
    51
  changes name, 15, 44
  converts to Islam, 43–44
  convicted of draft evasion,
    63, 65
  death threats against, 46, 51
  education, 18, 24
  Golden Gloves, 23, 29
  introduction to boxing, 22
  marriages, 42, 66, 116
  professional fights vs.
    Berbick, Trevor, 117–18
    Bonavena, Oscar, 83
    Chuvalo, George, 62, 72
    Cooper, Henry, 41, 62
    Evangelista, Alfredo, 109–
      10
    Foley, Zora, 65
    Foreman, George, 95–102
    Frazier, Joe, 84, 88, 92,
      104–5
    Holmes, Larry, 116
    Hunsaker, Tunney, 38
    Liston, Charles "Sonny,"
      46–49
    London, Brian, 62
    Marciano, Rocky 72–73
    Mildenberger, Karl, 62
    Moore, Archie, 38–39
    Norton, Ken, 89–90, 91,
      105–6
    Patterson, Floyd, 53
    Quarry, Jerry, 81–82
    Spinks, Leon, 111–13,
      114–15
    Terrell, Ernie, 11, 62
  Williams, Cleveland, 11
  refuses army induction, 11–
    13, 57, 63
  suffers from Parkinson's syn-
    drome, 116, 118, 119
  wins Olympic gold medal,
    31–32
Arum, Robert, 66, 68, 74

Basilio, Carmen, 38
Benton, George, 113, 114
Berbick, Trevor, 117, 118
Big Time Buck White (Brown),
  69
Black Muslims. See Nation of
  Islam
Bonavena, Oscar, 83
Boxing
  brain damage caused by, 119
  organized crime in, 32
  role of manager in, 32
  sparring, 36
  staged fights, 72
  weight classes, 27
Boyd, Belinda (second wife),
  66, 104
Braddock, James J., 106
Brown, Drew "Bundini," 11,
  49, 78
Brown, Oscar, Jr., 69

Cady, Steve, 82, 120
Chuvalo, George, 62, 72
Clay, Cassius, Sr. (father), 15
Clay, Cassius Marcellus (aboli-
  tionist), 24, 25
Clay, Cassius Marcellus, Jr. See
  Ali, Muhammad
Clay, Henry, 24
Clay, Odessa Grady (mother),
  15
Clay, Rudolph Valentino
  (brother), 15, 17

Cooper, Henry, 41, 62
Corbett, "Gentleman Jim," 27

D'Amato, Cus, 34
Dempsey, Jack, 27, 98, 105,
  107
Dundee, Angelo, 38, 46, 49,
  79, 100
Durham, Yank, 74, 85

Ellis, Jimmy, 71
Evangelista, Alfredo, 109, 110,
  112

Faversham, Bill, 35
Foley, Zora, 65
Foreman, George, 72, 89, 92,
  97, 98, 99, 100, 101, 102
Frazier, Joe, 71, 74, 83, 85, 86,
  87, 88, 89, 92, 104, 105

Golden Gloves tournaments,
  23, 29
Greatest: My Own Story, The,
  69
Greatest, The (film), 111

Hofheinz, Roy, 74
Holmes, Larry, 116
Houston, Texas, 11, 12, 62
Hunsaker, Tunney, 38

Jim Crow laws, 17
Johnson, Jack, 27, 53

King, Don, 96
King, Martin Luther, Jr., 69
Kinshasa, Zaire, 95, 96, 98
Kirk, Claude, 74
Ku Klux Klan, 18

LeDoux, Scott, 112
Lincoln, Abraham, 24, 25

Liston, Charles "Sonny," 38, 39, 42, 46, 47, 48, 49, 51, 52, 97
London, Brian, 62
Louis, Joe, 27, 56, 109
Louisville, Kentucky, 15, 16, 17, 21, 22, 23, 29, 33, 34, 38, 62
Louisville Millionaires, 35, 46, 53, 55, 65

McDonald, Bill, 45, 46
Maddox, Lester, 75
Madison Square Garden, 84, 92, 96, 99, 102
Mailer, Norman, 97
Malcolm X, 45, 51
Marciano, Rocky, 27, 28, 34, 72, 73
Marcos, Ferdinand, 104
Martin, Joe, 22, 24, 28, 33, 35
Massell, Sam, 75
Mildenberger, Karl, 62
Mobutu, Joseph, 95, 96
Moore, Archie, 34, 35, 36, 38, 39
Muhammad (founder of Islam), 43
Muhammad Ali Professional Sports, Inc., 116
Muhammad, Elijah, 43, 51, 53, 57, 63, 104

Muhammad, Herbert, 53, 65, 66, 68, 74, 96, 116
Muhammad, Wallace, 107, 109

Nation of Islam, 43, 44, 45, 51, 53, 57, 63, 65, 107
Newmann, Randy, 110
New York Times, 82, 91, 105, 110, 120
Nilon, Jack, 41
Norton, Ken, 89, 90, 91, 97, 105, 106, 112

Olympic Games (1960), 31–32

Pacheco, Ferdie, 79, 110, 111
Pastrano, William, 38
Patterson, Floyd, 42, 53, 97
Pelé, 60
Pietrzyskowski, Zbigniew, 31, 32
Porche, Veronica (third wife), 104, 116
Punch-drunk syndrome, 119

Quarry, Jerry, 72, 75, 77, 81

Requiem for a Heavyweight (Serling), 38
Reynolds, William, 33, 34, 35
Rivers, Mendel, 58
Robinson, Sugar Ray, 33

Rodriguez, Luis, 38
Roi, Sonji (first wife), 42, 51, 66
Roman, Joe "King," 97

Schmeling, Max, 107
Smith, Harold, 116, 117
Smith, "Lightning" Bob, 112
Smith, Red, 93, 105
Solomon, Sam, 113, 114
Spinks, Leon, 111–14
Spinks, Michael, 112
Stoner, Fred, 23, 24, 28, 29, 35
Sullivan, John L., 27

Terrell, Ernie, 11, 12, 62
Till, Emmett, 18, 20
Tunney, Gene, 27, 99, 105, 107

Universal military draft, 55, 56

Vietnam War, 56, 57, 59, 69, 73

Wallace, William, 90
Williams, Cleveland, 11, 12
Williams, John Bell, 74
Willis, Johnny, 20, 21
World Boxing Association (WBA), 63, 71
World Boxing Council (WBC), 71

PICTURE CREDITS

———————•❦•———————

JACK RUMMEL is a free-lance writer who lives in Hoboken, New Jersey. He is also the author of *Langston Hughes* in the BLACK AMERICANS OF ACHIEVEMENT series published by Chelsea House.

NATHAN IRVIN HUGGINS is W.E.B. Du Bois Professor of History and Director of the W.E.B. Du Bois Institute for Afro-American Research at Harvard University. He previously taught at Columbia University. Professor Huggins is the author of numerous books, including *Black Odyssey: The Afro-American Ordeal in Slavery, The Harlem Renaissance,* and *Slave and Citizen: The Life of Frederick Douglass.*